HEMINGWAY
IN AFRICA
THE LAST SAFARI

HEMINGWAY
IN AFRICA
THE LAST SAFARI

CHRISTOPHER
ONDAATJE

HarperCollins*PublishersLtd*

First edition

HarperCollins books may be purchased for educational, business,
or sales promotional use through our Special Markets Department.

HarperCollins Publishers Ltd.
2 Bloor Street East, 20th Floor
Toronto, Ontario, Canada
M4W 1A8

www.harpercanada.com

National Library of Canada Cataloguing in Publication

Ondaatje, Christopher
Hemingway in Africa: the last safari / Christopher Ondaatje.

Includes bibliographical references and index.
ISBN 0-00-200670-7

1. Hemingway, Ernest, 1898–1961—Journeys—Africa. 2. Authors,
American—20th century—Biography. I. Title.

PS3515.E37Z7487 2003   813'.52   C2003-902570-5

9 8 7 6 5 4 3 2 1

Designed and typeset by Libanus Press, Marlborough, England
Reprographics by B·A·S Printers Limited, Salisbury, England
Printed and bound by B·A·S Printers Limited, Salisbury, England

LITERARY ACKNOWLEDGEMENTS

The publishers have generously given permission to use quotations from the following copyrighted works written by Ernest Hemingway:

From "a.d. in Africa." Reprinted with permission of Scribner, an imprint of Simon & Schuster Adult Publishing Group, and the Hemingway Foreign Rights Trust, from *By-line: Ernest Hemingway*, edited by William White. Copyright 1934 by Ernest Hemingway. Copyright renewed © 1962 by Mary Hemingway and By-Line Ernest Hemingway, Inc. Copyright outside the United States: © Hemingway Foreign Rights Trust. Originally appeared in *Esquire* magazine, April 1934.

From "Black Novel a Storm Center." Reprinted with permission of Scribner, an imprint of Simon & Schuster Adult Publishing Group, and the Hemingway Foreign Rights Trust, from *Ernest Hemingway: Dateline: Toronto*, edited by William White. Copyright © 1985 by Mary Hemingway, John Hemingway, Patrick Hemingway, and Gregory Hemingway. Originally appeared in *Toronto Star Weekly*, March 25 1922.

From *Ernest Hemingway: Selected Letters, 1917–1961*. Inside the United States: reprinted with permission of Scribner, an imprint of Simon & Schuster Adult Publishing Group, from *Ernest Hemingway: Selected Letters, 1917–1961*, edited by Carlos Baker. Copyright © 1981 The Ernest Hemingway Foundation, Inc. Outside the United States: reprinted with permission of Scribner, an imprint of Simon & Schuster Adult Publishing Group, and the Hemingway Foreign Rights Trust from *Ernest Hemingway: Selected Letters, 1917–1961*, edited by Carlos Baker. Copyright outside the United States: © Hemingway Foreign Rights Trust.

From *The Garden of Eden*. Inside the United Kingdom: From *The Garden of Eden* by Ernest Hemingway (Hamish Hamilton, 1987) copyright © 1986 by Mary Hemingway, John Hemingway, Patrick Hemingway and Gregory Hemingway. Reproduced by permission of Penguin Books Ltd. Outside the United Kingdom: Copyright © 1986 by Mary Hemingway, John Hemingway, Patrick Hemingway and Gregory Hemingway. Reprinted with permission of Scribner, an imprint of Simon & Schuster Adult Publishing Group, from *The Garden of Eden* by Ernest Hemingway.

From *Green Hills of Africa*. Inside the United Kingdom: extract from *Green Hills of Africa* by Ernest Hemingway published by Jonathan Cape. Used by permission of The Random House Group Limited. Outside the United Kingdom: reprinted with permission of Scribner, an imprint of Simon & Schuster Adult Publishing Group, from *Green Hills of Africa* by Ernest Hemingway. Copyright 1935 by Charles Scribner's Sons. Copyright renewed © 1963 by Mary Hemingway.

From Ernest Hemingway's Nobel Prize Acceptance Speech, November 1954.

From "Notes on Dangerous Game." Reprinted with permission of Scribner, an imprint of Simon & Schuster Adult Publishing Group, and the Hemingway Foreign Rights Trust, from *By-line: Ernest Hemingway*, edited by William White. Copyright 1934 by Ernest Hemingway. Copyright renewed © 1962 by Mary Hemingway and By-Line Ernest Hemingway, Inc. Copyright outside the United States: © Hemingway Foreign Rights Trust. Originally appeared in *Esquire* magazine, July 1934.

From *The Old Man and the Sea*. Inside the United Kingdom: extract from *The Old Man and the Sea* by Ernest Hemingway published by Jonathan Cape. Used by permission of The Random House Group Limited. Outside the United Kingdom: reprinted with permission of Scribner, an imprint of Simon & Schuster Adult Publishing Group, from *The Old Man and the Sea* by Ernest Hemingway. Copyright 1952 by Ernest Hemingway. Copyright renewed © 1980 by Mary Hemingway.

From "Safari" by Ernest Hemingway (*Look* magazine, Vol. 18, No. 2, January 26 1954).

From "Shootism versus Sport." Reprinted with permission of Scribner, an imprint of Simon & Schuster Adult Publishing Group, and the Hemingway Foreign Rights Trust, from *By-line: Ernest Hemingway*, edited by William White. Copyright 1934 by Ernest Hemingway. Copyright renewed © 1962 by Mary Hemingway and By-Line Ernest Hemingway, Inc. Copyright outside the United States: © Hemingway Foreign Rights Trust. Originally appeared in *Esquire* magazine, June 1934.

From "The Short Happy Life of Francis Macomber." Inside the United Kingdom: extract from "The Short Happy Life of Francis Macomber." by Ernest Hemingway published by Jonathan Cape.

For David, Sarah and Jans

PHOTOGRAPHIC ACKNOWLEDGEMENTS

The author and publishers express their thanks to the following sources for permission to reproduce illustrated material. In the event that any omissions have occurred proper acknowledgements will be made in future editions.

Roxann E. Livingston/The Earl Theisen Archive: jacket photograph, pp. 164, 181, 182, and 191. © 2003 Earl Theisen/Roxann E. Livingston/JFK Library
Images may not be reused or reassigned to other publishers without written permission of the Roxann E. Livingston/The Earl Theisen Archive.

Peter Beard/A+C Anthology: pp. 44, 46, 48, 66 and 175.

Yousuf Karsh, Camera Press London: p. 216.

Getty Images/Hulton: pp. 20, 24, 36, 37, 40, 96, 134, 142, 144, 196 and 218.

Royal Geographical Society: p. 18.

Ernest Hemingway Collection, John F. Kennedy Library, Boston, USA: pp. 22, 25, 24, 34, 35, 54, 61, 63, 92, 123, 131, 132, 148, 151, 153, 171, 194 and 203. (Photographs on pp. 34 and 54 by Helen Breaker, Paris.)

Christopher Ondaatje © The Ondaatje Foundation: pp. 4, 10, 12, 15, 16, 30, 33, 38, 43, 50, 51, 52, 57, 58, 68, 70, 72, 75, 76, 79, 85, 89, 94, 99, 102, 105, 106, 111, 112, 116, 118, 121, 146, 160, 162, 167, 168, 172, 178, 187, 201, 206, 208, 212, 214, 224, 227, 228, 230, 236 and 238.

CONTENTS

AUTHOR'S ACKNOWLEDGEMENTS

Besides Ernest Hemingway's own prolific writings, an enormous amount has been written about him, and also about many of the people (such as Karen Blixen) mentioned in this book. In selecting what to read from this material, I owe a great deal to the superior knowledge of a number of Hemingway scholars, duly credited in the Bibliography, who put me on the right track for understanding Hemingway in Africa.

Controversy is unavoidable with Hemingway. I have tried to read and learn with an open mind – if there is such a thing – and to temper my undoubted enthusiasm with detachment. My chief hope is to persuade readers to take seriously views that some think misguided or even idiotic: principally that Africa was a key influence on Hemingway's life and writings.

I would like to thank the following people for their invaluable help and advice in the research and preparation of this manuscript: Rosemary Aubert, Fiona Bondzio, Maryan Gibson and Dinny Gollop. Kelly Jones was remarkably patient in securing permissions to quote from Hemingway; Michael Berry and Michael Mitchell helped with the book's design and production. I could not have produced this book without them.

Mangati woman in southern Tanzania.

FOREWORD

"The Snows of Kilimanjaro" is one of the world's classic short stories, and one of the most famous fictions written by Ernest Hemingway. It appeared in 1936, two years after Hemingway returned from his first African safari, when he was at the height of his literary and worldly success. Yet its central character is a wealthy writer on safari who is a failure. The gangrene in his leg forces him to admit that he has frittered away his literary talent on a life of luxury and will now never produce anything enduring, any writing with the radiance of the snows at the summit of nearby Mount Kilimanjaro. Despite his own undoubted achievements as a writer, which in 1954 won him the Nobel prize for literature, Hemingway put himself and his fears for the future deeply into this mid-life story. And it does indeed appear to have foreshadowed his literary decline in the 1940s and 1950s, and his subsequent suicide.

All this is familiar to readers of Hemingway. Not so well known is that his love affair with Africa began when he was a child in Illinois and lasted right up to his death. As a boy he was thrilled by Theodore Roosevelt's African safari and books like *The Man-Eaters of Tsavo*; in his twenties, his first professional book review was of a French novel about Africa by a black writer; his first safari produced a major book, *Green Hills of Africa*, while his second safari twenty years later led to a sprawling "African Journal," published posthumously as *True at First Light*; and this is not to mention some excellent shorter pieces of fiction and non-fiction with an African theme, including the two celebrated short stories, "The Snows of Kilimanjaro" and "The Short Happy Life of Francis Macomber." Even though he almost died at the end of his second safari in a plane crash which left his health in a parlous state, still he wanted to return to Africa for a third safari. Clearly Africa bewitched Hemingway.

Young Masai morani *watering cattle.*

Christopher Ondaatje's *Hemingway in Africa* investigates this fascination with a charming mixture of perceptive analysis of Hemingway's African writings and personal insight into the mind of a complex and driven individual whom Ondaatje both admires and deplores. While others have written about Hemingway and Africa, Ondaatje is the first to pursue Hemingway *in* Africa, by following in his footsteps on his two safaris in Kenya, Tanzania and Uganda, as he did in a previous book *Journey to the Source of the Nile* which followed the great Victorian explorers of East Africa. Ondaatje's own journey through the post-colonial Africa of our time is interwoven with Hemingway's imperial progress; and the one intriguingly illuminates the other. As he remarks of Hemingway: "Certainly he was no explorer, not a man like Livingstone or Burton always looking for new discoveries, usually in uncharted territory, and motivated by a certain necessary humility. Yet he was more than a mere adventurer. As a *writer* about Africa, I think Hemingway deserves to be called an explorer, even if he was only an adventurer in his travels and personal life on safari."

Both hunter and quarry in this book are men of action and affairs, successful risk-takers in their chosen fields. But both are also romantics. The tension between realism and romance, which drives both worldly and artistic achievement, makes *Hemingway in Africa* an absorbing read as well as a significant contribution to Hemingway studies.

ANDREW ROBINSON
Literary Editor
The Times Higher Education Supplement
October 2003

Masai children tending goats.

INTRODUCTION

Kilimanjaro is a snow covered mountain 19,710 feet high,
and is said to be the highest mountain in Africa. Its western
summit is called "Ngàje Ngài," the House of God. Close to
the western summit there is the dried and frozen carcass of
a leopard. No one has explained what the leopard was
seeking at that altitude.

ERNEST HEMINGWAY
"The Snows of Kilimanjaro"[1]

Leopards are the most dangerous, secretive and alluring of all the African cats. Perhaps it is their combination of indolent beauty and deadly cunning that attracts many of us so strongly. Or possibly it is their solitariness, for leopards are anti-social creatures, seen together only during the mating season, and unlike lions they hunt alone and almost exclusively at night. For anyone who likes a personal challenge, trying to catch a glimpse of this unique creature is as irresistible as the sirens' song. No wonder Ernest Hemingway, in his best-known story about Africa, made a leopard into a tantalizing artistic symbol.

The leopard carcass mentioned at the beginning of "The Snows of Kilimanjaro" was no fiction. It was found in 1926 by an English mountaineer, Donald Latham, during his climb to the summit of Kilimanjaro. Latham published photographs of the carcass on a pile of rocks and of a bearer proudly holding it above his head, and in his

Hemingway sets up the presence of the leopard near the summit of Mount
Kilimanjaro in the prologue to "The Snows of Kilimanjaro" as a riddle that
the reader must try to answer through the tale that follows.

The leopard carcass mentioned at the beginning of "The Snows of Kilimanjaro" was no fiction. It was found in 1926 by an English mountaineer, Donald Latham, during his climb to the summit.

description of the ascent he wrote: "A remarkable discovery was the remains of a leopard, sun-dried and frozen, right at the crater rim. The beast must have wandered there and died of exposure."[2] Latham thought that the leopard had been hunting, had lost its way in a blizzard and had been driven up the mountain to escape the cold. Hemingway, however, offers no explanation. Rather, he sets up the presence of the leopard near the summit in the prologue to his story as a riddle that the reader must try to answer through the tale that follows.

Kilimanjaro has had a mystical significance to man ever since he first set eyes on it. The Masai people view the mountain as holy, and the Chaga, the tribe who live on its slopes, believe its heights to be the home of Ruwa, the sun god, the great protector and provider who created nature, man and beasts. The high, flat summit known as Kibo is particularly revered by the Chaga, because it is thought to bring rain. When they wish to pray to Ruwa, they face the mountain; and their dead are buried with heads pointing towards it.

In "The Snows of Kilimanjaro," Harry, a writer on safari, is dying in the shadow of the great peak. Waiting for the plane that is his only hope of rescue, he dwells on his past and the mistakes he has made. Through his sniping at his wife and his recollections of Europe, the reader learns of Harry's marriage to a rich woman he does not love, of the gangrenous leg that is going to kill him, and of his intense wartime and post-war experiences that will now never be put into print because Harry has betrayed his writing talent for a life of luxury.

Though Kilimanjaro broods over the story, the leopard is mentioned only once. Still, its image haunted me, along with many other of the story's images. "The Snows of Kilimanjaro" and its origins in Hemingway's life, seemed worthy of fresh investigation. Together with Karen Blixen's *Out of Africa* and Beryl Markham's *West with the Night*, Hemingway's story is at the centre of an extensive collection of books, maps, photographs and articles about East Africa that I have accumulated since the mid-1980s while travelling there in search of wildlife and the sources of the Nile. Although the story is brief compared to Hemingway's novels, it is perfect. It encapsulates the enduring themes of the Hemingway opus: how a man can be heroic in the face of slaughter and death; how he can remain true to a personal vision when everyday life conspires to cloud it; and how a writer's life must inspire his writings. For as the Hemingway scholar Jeffrey Meyers writes in *Hemingway: Life into Art*, "One of Hemingway's fundamental aesthetic principles was that fiction must be based on actual experience."[3] Why is Hemingway's most penetrating look at a writer's failure set in Africa? What exactly was Hemingway's relationship with Africa? What was he seeking there?

I decided to visit Hemingway country in Kenya, Tanzania (Tanganyika in Hemingway's time) and Uganda. By following in his footsteps and experiencing at first hand the places he wrote about on his two safaris, in 1933–34 and 1953–54, I sensed that one could understand Hemingway's attraction to Africa in a deeper way than his many biographers, excellent

Ernest Hemingway, seen here in the 1920s, was the first great American literary celebrity of the twentieth century.

though their books are about his life in America and Europe. On my safari, I would stop where he stopped and look where he looked, in a quest for the heart of his strange and profound affection for Africa. Hemingway has been much analysed over the decades since his death, but in my view Africa's role in his life and work remains intriguing and under-explored territory.

✳   ✳   ✳

Ernest Hemingway was the first great American literary celebrity of the twentieth century. When he shot himself in 1961, he was an international legend: the white-bearded face of 'Papa' Hemingway was recognized the world over without a caption. Countless magazine articles had chronicled the adventures of the hard-drinking, tough-talking, much-married action man, and almost as many literary studies had considered the psychology behind the work, his place as a modernist writer, and the anatomy of his pared-down style. After his death, Hemingway became an industry. His childhood home in Oak Park, Illinois, and his houses in Key West and in Cuba, are national monuments. Any bar in Paris or Madrid or Havana where he might once have dropped in for a whisky or four proudly displays the fact. Regarded as classic texts in every American high school, his works still inspire comment from leading scholars, while competitions to imitate his inimitable prose are inundated with entries.

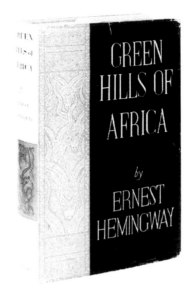

Green Hills of Africa, *which recounts Hemingway's first African safari in 1933–34, remains underrated.*

But despite the persistence of Hemingway mania, Hemingway in Africa is relatively neglected both by the reading public and by scholars. His two African short stories, "The Snows of Kilimanjaro" and "The Short Happy Life of Francis Macomber," are rightly judged to be among his best work, but his non-fiction book *Green Hills of Africa*, which recounts his first safari, remains underrated, and the posthumously published *True at First Light*, about his second safari, is widely dismissed as the ramblings of an ageing and ailing man capable only of flashes of his former brilliance. Moreover, few seem to realize that embedded within another posthumously published work, *The Garden of Eden*, is an emotional short story of an African elephant hunt. Its inclusion within an experimental, even "kinky"[4] book shows that Hemingway never got Africa out of his system. For him, Africa was a readily available metaphor for escape, as well as something much more. Through all the adventures, travels, romances and achievements of Hemingway's early career, Africa remained a constant dream. He fell in love with the *idea* of Africa long before he fell in love with Africa. When,

Hemingway's family. An intense love of nature was first instilled in him when he was a child living in an affluent suburb of Chicago. His father brought up his children to appreciate and observe the natural world, and at that time such appreciation included hunting. Above: Ernest on his father's knee.

at thirty-four, he finally made the journey to Kenya and Tanganyika, he was bewitched by its exotic landscape. He longed to return almost before he had left. Another twenty years would pass before he did, and that second safari came close to killing him; nevertheless, he wrote of it as one of the happiest times in his life.

An intense love of nature was first instilled in him when he was a child living in an affluent suburb of Chicago. The 'wilds' in which he spent his summers learning to hunt and shoot were those of rural Michigan. His father brought up his children to appreciate and observe the natural world, and at that time such appreciation included hunting as it still does in some minds. Field trips to study the local area were complemented by expeditions to Chicago's Field Museum of Natural History to look at foreign animals on display. The boy Ernest was particularly entranced by the stuffed elephants brought back from Africa in the early years of the century by the explorer and conservationist Carl Akeley. Akeley had filmed gorillas in the wild and reputedly killed a wounded and aggressive leopard with his bare hands; he was the stuff boyhood heroes are made of. As a direct result, Hemingway became intrigued by the exotic and dangerous prospect of hunting big game.

In 1909 Theodore Roosevelt's term as president ended and he went on an African safari. It was his first big expedition after leaving the White House and marked the fulfilment of a long-held ambition. Protector of the Grand Canyon and a leading conservationist of his time, Roosevelt is credited with founding the environmental movement in the United States. However, his concern for the natural world did nothing to diminish his passion for the hunt, which was one of the great pleasures in his life. His huge entourage on safari included his son Kermit and several naturalists. They made use of scores of African porters and trackers and were accompanied by all the finest 'white hunters,' one of whom, Philip Percival, would later lead both of Hemingway's safaris. Roosevelt's stated purpose was to collect specimens for the national museum in Washington, DC, but despite its educational aim, the trip became known primarily for the sheer scale of

the slaughter it visited on Kenya's wildlife. More than a thousand animals were killed, 296 of them by Roosevelt himself. The level of killing was shocking, but the safari brought huge international publicity to the area, which softened the criticisms of those who found the expedition's death tally hard to stomach.

Roosevelt was Hemingway's childhood idol, and the young Ernest – his interest in Africa sparked by Akeley's collection of animals in Chicago – devoured the numerous magazine articles describing the 1909 safari. Roosevelt's books, *African Game Trails* (1910) and *Through the Brazilian Wilderness* (1914), had an honoured place next to Akeley's memoir, *In Brightest Africa* (1923), on his shelves. Roosevelt inspired Hemingway to such an extent that, at sixteen, he was quite certain he wanted to be a pioneer or an explorer in one of the last great frontiers – Africa, South America or the Arctic, north of Hudson Bay. He already believed that the hiking he did in the spring, and his farm and woodland work in the summer, would help develop resourcefulness and self-reliance for his future adventurous pursuits.

In 1921, after becoming a reporter and correspondent and moving to Paris, Hemingway had his first encounter with fiction about Africa. He was fascinated by *Batouala*, a newly published first novel by an unknown black French writer, René Maran, which had just won the Goncourt Prize. The book was the subject of Hemingway's inaugural professional

Left: In 1909 Theodore Roosevelt's term as president ended and he went on an African safari. It was his first big expedition after leaving the White House and marked the fulfilment of a long-held ambition.

Above: Roosevelt was Hemingway's childhood idol, and the young Ernest devoured the numerous magazine articles describing the 1909 safari.

Above: Batouala, *a first novel by an unknown black French writer, René Maran, was the subject of Hemingway's inaugural professional book review, published in the* Toronto Star *in 1922.*

book review, published in the *Toronto Star* in 1922. It is significant not only for being a first for him but also because it hints at the qualities we now associate with Hemingway's own fiction. At this early stage, Hemingway had yet to establish his own style, and the myth of "Papa"

Hemingway was a long way off, but his review of *Batouala* shows the excitement of its writer's imagination stimulated by a novelist's convincing picture of an unfamiliar, enticing world.

*   *   *

Batouala is a tribal chief in French-ruled central Africa whose favourite wife, the first of nine, is stolen from him by his best friend, the handsome, virile Bissibingui. Batouala plots to kill Bissibingui, but his spear thrust misses and instead Batouala himself is fatally mauled by a leopard. Hemingway's praise focuses on Maran's ability to write from experience in an unaffected way that enables the reader to relive that experience fully in his own mind. "The reader gets a picture of a native village seen by the big-whited eyes, felt by the pink palms, and the broad, flat, naked feet of the African native himself. You smell the smells of the village, you eat its food, you see the white man as the black man sees him, and after you have lived in the village you die there." In *Batouala*, writes Hemingway, the reader is given "the facts by a man who has seen them, in a plain, unimpassioned statement." At the end, the dying Batouala is prostrate in his hut almost alone, abandoned by the village sorcerer. According to Hemingway, "Batouala lies there feverish and thirsty, dying, while his mangy dog licks at his wounds. And while he lies there, you feel the thirst and the fever and the rough, moist tongue of the dog." It was a simple enough story, "but when you have read it, you have seen Batouala, and that makes it a great novel."[5]

In all of Hemingway's African writing, there is a startling juxtaposition of the world he came from and the world he has come to. The differences between the two are not something Hemingway wastes words in expounding, yet the dichotomy between the familiar and the foreign is always implied. This dichotomy is evident, too, in the work of Maran, who was not in fact an African but a Caribbean-born French colonial servant posted in Africa. Maran's writing career covers virtually the exact same period as Hemingway's, and it is interesting to compare their two lives, which could hardly have been more different.

Maran was born in Martinique in 1887, twelve years before Hemingway. After completing his baccalaureat in France, he went to Bangui (capital of today's Central African Republic) as a minor official. There his white colleagues looked down on him and resented his sharing of their privileges, while the Africans regarded him with suspicion for having joined the colonial establishment. Unlike the young Hemingway, who was surrounded by writers in Paris such as Gertrude Stein, James Joyce, Ezra Pound and Scott Fitzgerald, Maran had no support when he began work on his novel in an attempt to forget his struggles and loneliness. It took him six years to write, but when it won the Prix Goncourt, Maran became famous overnight. However, while Hemingway's early novel, *The Sun Also Rises*, brought him nothing but advantages – high sales, recognition, critical respect – *Batouala* came close to ruining its author's career. Its indictment of French colonialism in Africa created heated controversy: black critics hailed Maran as a hero and spokesman, while white French critics upbraided him for his ingratitude and lack of patriotism, and a member of the French parliament even demanded that sanctions be levelled against him. Eventually the vituperation within the colonial service became so fierce that Maran resigned from his position in 1923 and returned to France (travelling via the British colony of Nigeria to avoid French officialdom). He later claimed that after *Batouala* his reputation was such that publishers put a tacit ban on his work.

But he continued to write, working on poetry and contributing to periodicals. From the late 1920s, as Hemingway's literary star continued to rise with the publication and extraordinarily favourable reception of *A Farewell to Arms*, Maran was able to publish further novels, though without much fanfare. In the Second World War, as the now-legendary Hemingway returned to Europe as *Collier's* front-line correspondent, Maran's colour, stature and marriage to a white Frenchwoman brought him to the attention of the Gestapo. He courageously refused to write pro-Negro, anti-American or anti-French propaganda for the Nazis and remained devoted to the Free French cause throughout the occupation. Miraculously, he survived the war.

Introspective, reserved and unwilling to promote himself, Maran did not receive, before his death in 1960, the acclaim he knew he deserved. He believed passionately in his work as a "social writer," and spent his life and career in a quiet struggle against the racism and hypocrisy of those in power. Hemingway, of course, was the antithesis, consorting with the rich, powerful and glamorous and actively creating his own myth, courting fame to the point where the myth came close to eclipsing the work.

It is impossible to consider Hemingway's Africa separate from such colonial issues, complex as those issues have always been – and certainly still are in today's post-colonial world. The Africas of the great Victorian explorers, of Carl Akeley and Theodore Roosevelt, of René Maran, Karen Blixen and Beryl Markham, of Hemingway's first safari in 1933 and his second in 1953, the Africa of my own first safari and of this, my last – are all different, each of them, as we come nearer to our own time, further away from the tribal kingdoms and natural wilderness of Africa that met the eyes of David Livingstone. Yet something of the original Africa, and of colonial Africa before it went irreparably wrong, does remain. This was the Africa that Hemingway sought and found. And this was what I too went after, on safari in Hemingway's footsteps.

CHAPTER 1

Preparations

Something, or something awful or something wonderful
was certain to happen on every day in this part of Africa.
Every morning when you woke it was as exciting as though
you were going to compete in a downhill ski race or drive
a bobsled on a fast run. Something, you knew, would
happen and usually before eleven o'clock. I never knew of
a morning in Africa when I woke that I was not happy.

ERNEST HEMINGWAY
True at First Light[1]

To follow in the footsteps of an earlier traveller requires knowing
not only where that traveller went and when, but also why. One must
balance the known facts with one's own hunches and speculations. To be
accurate and relevant, all "footsteps journeys" must begin with detailed
research into what has been written on the subject. One of the most
challenging aspects of planning my 1996 journey in the footsteps of Sir
Richard Burton in search of the source of the Nile was that so many of
the place-names had changed since the 1850s. This was not a problem
with the Hemingway trip. My re-creation of Hemingway's travels in
Africa began with detailed notes about every African town mentioned in
any book by and about Hemingway that I could find. Using *Green Hills
of Africa* and the unpublished journal of Hemingway's second wife,

*Mombasa. The masses of people streaming to work (many disgorging from the
Likoni ferry that crosses the narrow estuary to the main harbour in the north)
and the hundreds of cars and smoke-belching old lorries, made for slow going.*

Pauline Pfeiffer, it was relatively easy to learn the place-names of stops on the first safari. Similarly, using *True at First Light* and the journal of Hemingway's fourth wife, Mary Welsh, I was able to trace the second Hemingway safari. Then, with a modern map of East Africa, I plotted the first journey and superimposed the second onto it. I decided to make a single safari, covering both of Hemingway's trips in one go – a 7300-kilometre journey.

I did not have Hemingway's privilege of being waited on in camp hand and foot, but I did have the advantage of having been to some of these East African towns and cities several times before. When planning, I took into consideration that Hemingway's two safaris were quite different from each other. The first, which began in December 1933, was truly a hunting trip and involved a good deal of moving about in the bush. Twenty years later, not surprisingly, an older and less agile Hemingway spent more time simply enjoying his camp at Tsavo, near the foot of Mount Kilimanjaro. In the end, my plan was simple: follow as closely as possible the route Hemingway took around Kenya and Tanganyika on his first safari, then rest for a few days near Lake Naivasha in Kenya before moving on to the Tsavo region to investigate the second safari.

Hemingway's first African journey took him in a large circle. The passage from Mombasa to Nairobi was made in a day with no hunting, then he went down to Arusha in Tanganyika and on to Lake Manyara, where the safari proper began. Thereafter he made his way around the Masai Steppe, camping at Babati, moving steadily east through Kolo, Goima, Kibaya, on to Handeni and finally to Tanga and the Kenyan coast, where he spent a few days fishing before heading home to Key West.

The first safari was originally to have been a boys-only affair. The initial line-up included Charles Thompson, who was a friend from Key West, the poet Archibald MacLeish and another friend, Henry Strater. MacLeish and Strater backed out in the planning stages, ostensibly for financial and domestic reasons, although some Hemingway biographers

Hemingway's first African journey in 1933–34 took him in a large circle.

have suggested the pair feared that their friend's competitive ego would turn the safari into a three-month test of machismo measured by the size of horns and quality of skins collected. A pretty astute prediction, as things turned out. Hemingway may have been disappointed that his other friends could not join him, but by the time his party set off, he was quite reconciled to the idea of a smaller group – himself, Thompson and his wife Pauline.

He was determined to give Pauline, the only woman among the trackers, gun bearers, cooks and hunters – and no natural tomboy – a happy

experience. Even with today's modern camping equipment, a safari is an uncomfortable affair, and it is to Pauline's credit that she willingly went along. She and Ernest were probably already having marital difficulties at this time, though, and the trip may have been part of her strategy to hang on to her husband. The two had met eight years earlier in Paris when she was working for *Vogue* and Ernest was married to Hadley Richardson. Pauline and her sister, Virginia, asked to be introduced to the famous Hemingways and quickly became part of their Paris set. Small and slender with a bright, impish face, Pauline was at first a friend of both husband and wife. But the balance soon altered. She was strongly attracted to the young and handsome Ernest and a frank admirer of his work. Well read and quick witted, she was a good critic and full of praise for his talent. By the time the three of them set off for Austria to spend Christmas of 1925 together, Pauline was very much in love and determined to become Hemingway's wife. Later on, Hemingway came to believe that his split from his first wife had been a great mistake; he idealized Hadley and their early life in Paris in his late memoir, *A Moveable Feast*. But there is no doubt that he loved his second wife Pauline, too.

*　*　*

Seventeen days after leaving Marseilles on November 22 1933, the small Hemingway party set foot in Mombasa. Bernice Kert, in her book *The*

Hemingway met Pauline Pfeiffer (above) in 1925 when she was working in Paris for Vogue. *Later on, Hemingway came to believe that his split from his first wife Hadley Richardson (opposite) had been a great mistake.*

Hemingway Women, describes their appearance. "Ernest put on a wide-brimmed Stetson and rolled up his shirt sleeves for the disembarking. Pauline, not to be outdone, wore an ankle-length white dress and gloves and carried a ruffled white parasol. 'Pauline and I looked like missionaries,' recalled Charles [Thompson], 'while Ernest had the distinct look of a whisky drummer.'"[2] Kenya's port city in the 1930s was bustling but beautiful. The intense cornflower blue of the sea arced around an ideal harbour – Vasco da Gama stopped in Mombasa on his famous Indian voyage in 1498 – and the old Portuguese fortress overlooked the narrow streets of the town, "all built from coral-rock, in pretty shades of buff, rose, and ochre," as Karen Blixen describes Mombasa in *Out of Africa*. For her the city had "all the look of a picture of paradise painted

35

Seventeen days after sailing from Marseilles on November 22 1933, the small Hemingway party set foot in Mombasa.

by a small child . . . . The air is salt here, the breeze brings in every day fresh supplies of brine from the East, and the soil itself is salted so that very little grass grows, and the ground is bare like a dancing-floor."[3]

Nearly seventy years later, the Mombasa that greeted me could hardly have changed more. The scent in the air was more diesel than salt. Enormous white buildings had largely replaced the buff and rose-coloured ones, and overlooking the narrow streets now was not so much the old fortress but the high-rise structures of commerce.

Though tempted to use the excellent safari team that had accompanied me on my previous African expeditions, for this journey I wanted to do something different, to start over with a new perspective. So, as well as three support staff, I hired the experienced safari guide and hunter Joerg Bondzio. Of German and Italian extraction, Joerg has lived in both Kenya and Tanzania. We employed two Land Rovers. Joerg drove one,

The Kipevu causeway links Old Mombasa to the African mainland.

with Andrea Kinyozi – a Tanzanian guide who had travelled with Joerg before – and me as passengers; while a Kenyan guide, with the single name Philies, drove the other vehicle, in which also travelled Ernest Ombuya, a cook who worked for Joerg's father-in-law in Nairobi. Determined to be as independent as possible, we took all our tenting equipment and food with us.

Joerg had done a lot of reading about Hemingway in Africa before my arrival in Kenya and had charted a proposed journey from the maps I had given him of Hemingway's safaris. The other men knew very little about Hemingway, and part of the pleasure of the trip was sharing our knowledge as we went along. At breakfast before setting out or at dinner

Beneath the sticky heat of Mombasa there always lurks an ominous sense of danger; one is far more likely to notice armed police upon arrival than the shady mango trees that greeted the Hemingways when they reached the port in 1933.

around the camp-fire in the evening, we discussed the significance of the places where we stayed. As often as possible we camped where we thought the Hemingway party might have camped.

Unlike Hemingway and his wife Pauline, the post-colonial traveller in Africa does not feel the need to wear a costume. The cotton khaki shirts and trousers most people wear on safari today are simply cool, comfortable and capable of obscuring the fact that one is filthy for a good part of any safari, even though experienced trekkers wash their clothes as often as they can. I have an old felt hat that I bought some time ago in Montana. It was on my head when, at eight in the morning, we drove under the great crossed elephant tusks, symbol of Mombasa, that come to a pinnacle over the city's main east/west street. The masses of people streaming to work (many disgorging from the Likoni ferry that crosses the narrow estuary to the main harbour in the north) and the hundreds of cars and smoke-belching old lorries, made for slow going. Out of the humidity of the morning flashed a sudden downpour, but the people on foot merely quickened their pace, carrying furniture or briefcases and shielding their heads with the morning newspaper, apparently not caring that they were getting wet, perhaps even enjoying the cool respite from the heat. Everywhere were signs of urban lifestyle – casinos, restaurants, cinemas, banks and more banks.

Beneath the sticky heat of Mombasa there always lurks an ominous sense of danger; one is far more likely to notice armed police upon arrival than the shady mango trees that greeted the Hemingways. Of course, travelling in any third-world country is somewhat hazardous, and I am sure Hemingway too had to consider security. On his second safari, the Mau Mau, a secret society formed by members of the Kikuyu tribe in Kenya and sworn by oath to rid the country of white colonists – and of the many Africans who opposed the Mau Mau – were beginning to be a terrorist threat. In addition, there are always numerous tribal conflicts to consider. The traveller in East Africa must exercise a good deal of common sense and not look for trouble. Tribal animosities go back generations and it is best not to get in the way of them. I always take people along who can speak Swahili and talk our way out of any trouble.

In December 1933, Hemingway and his party spent the weekend in Mombasa before catching the train for the 530-kilometre journey inland to Nairobi. For him, rattling through the dust by train, big game easily visible from every window, the snow-topped peak of Kilimanjaro just visible like a distant promise, the journey must have been incredibly exciting.

Going by road was somewhat less so. The start of the Nairobi road out of Mombasa was as bad an arterial route as imaginable. Unpaved and potholed, it looked as if its construction had been started and then abandoned. There seemed to be more trucks than cars. At the side of the highway were great holes with heaps of mud beside them. According to Joerg, things had improved since the previous year, when the road had gullies in it during the heavy rains as high as our Land Rovers! Luckily

In December 1933, Hemingway and his party spent the weekend in Mombasa before catching the train for the 530-kilometre journey inland to Nairobi (above).

it was now dry as we travelled past small boutiques and dusty coconut plantations. Running parallel to the road was the track of the train that the Hemingway party took.

The Kenya-Uganda railway, which stretches from Mombasa to Lake Victoria, was considered to be one of the great imperial achievements of Queen Victoria's reign. But the five-and-a-half years that the mammoth project required were so fraught with difficulties that the railway gained a nickname, the Lunatic Express. When work began in 1895, the thousand imported workers – coolies from India experienced in building the railways of the subcontinent – brought with them a plethora of diseases, including syphilis, which rapidly worked their way through the indigenous population. The coolies and the African workers succumbed to malaria, pneumonia and amoebic dysentery in such numbers that by 1896 only half were healthy enough to work. Then there was a hold-up because the planned Macuba bridge, intended to link Mombasa island to the mainland, proved problematic. Perfect bridge-building timber grew well inland on the slopes of the Rift Valley. Of course transporting it to the site required a bridge – the very bridge that had yet to be built. Eventually, the timber had to be imported all the way from England, causing another costly delay. Then there were stoppages due to rivers in flood. But the railway track began to snake its way through the country, and by 1898, 160 kilometres of track had been laid. At Tsavo, however, there was a new and unexpected hold-up.

Man-eating lions. Two elusive man-eaters were on the rampage. They avoided the many traps set for them, spread fear throughout the camp, and humbled the hunters who came to Tsavo in hopes of picking up the hefty bounty on the beasts' heads. The bridge builders were terrified, forced to sleep in treetops or in railway carriages to escape the lions' night raids. By the end of that year, the marauders had killed twenty-eight coolies and scores of Africans. The workers would work no longer; many coolies demanded to be returned to India.

The Man-Eaters of Tsavo, published in 1907, which sold out five printings in twelve years, was another tale of African adventure devoured

J. H. Patterson, author of The Man-Eaters of Tsavo, *worked as an engineer on the Tsavo bridge in the 1890s. The lion is one of the two man-eaters he shot.*

by Hemingway as a boy. Its author, J. H. Patterson, a lieutenant colonel in the Indian army, worked as an engineer on the Tsavo bridge in the 1890s. He was deeply unpopular among the coolies for his harsh treatment of them, resented for his ruthless, uncompromising drive; indeed ultimately Patterson was so hated that the workers decided to kill him. However he received their open threat coolly, faced down the mob and, when the moment of danger had passed, announced that if the men would resume work, he would be willing to overlook their scheme to murder him. No surprise, perhaps, that this stubborn man should have been the person who eventually slew the man-eaters.

It had been a long reign of terror, but the end, when it came, was quick. Patterson got his chance soon after the workers' strike. One of the lions had been chased away from its kill – in this case a donkey – and was likely to return to resume feeding. Patterson waited three metres up a nearby tree and when the lion reappeared, pulled the trigger repeatedly until the beast was dead. A few weeks later he killed the second man-eater in similar circumstances, narrowly escaping death himself when the lion, wounded by the first shot, charged him and collapsed only feet away.

With the man-eaters out of the way, progress was steady. At last, in 1901, this extraordinary, 940-kilometre railway, which traversed every kind of terrain and climatic condition on its way to the largest lake in Africa, was finished. The opening of Kenya to European settlement could begin.

The first settlers, arriving before the First World War, were mostly from landed stock – aristocrats and gentlemen of independent means. They included sportsmen, adventurers, entrepreneurs and a few devoted naturalists; and their chief traits were the type of independence, tenacity, ambition and fearlessness that Hemingway admired. In *Happy Valley: The Story of the English in Kenya*, Nicholas Best describes those pioneering times:

> There were as yet few rules in Kenya. It was still frontier country, where people sank or swam according to their own ability, where money and position mattered little in the

scramble to survive against everything that nature could drop on them. Enormous areas of bush had to be cleared, trees felled, bore holes sunk, streams dammed, fields ploughed and irrigated, roads built, quarries dug, boulders shifted, shade trees planted and seed beds tenderly nursed. There was little time at first for social niceties.

Many early settlers were fugitives in disgrace from Edwardian society, exiled perhaps for losing too much at cards or for getting a debutante in foal, bringing with them the unmistakable stamp of the English upper classes and printing it firmly on new earth.[4]

The 1920s brought social change. The years of struggle to redevelop the land in the years immediately following the war were paying off. Settlers and ex-servicemen who had come in droves to find a better way of life could now afford a more leisurely, frivolous existence. Kenya was

An early picture of the author at the Muthaiga Country Club, built in 1913 in an exclusive part of Nairobi.

Hemingway's safari guide on his first trip, Philip Percival, was a successful farmer and also one of the greatest of the white hunters; and someone Hemingway was to admire for the rest of his life.

by no means immune to the jazz age, and characters such as Brett Ashley, the flamboyant anti-heroine of Hemingway's *The Sun Also Rises* – that chronicle of the aimless hedonism of the period – might not have looked or felt out of place in Kenya's 'white highlands' society. For the privileged members of the Muthaiga Country Club, built in 1913 in an exclusive part of Nairobi, life was one long party interrupted by the occasional shooting trip or fishing competition. Such was its reputation for pleasure-seeking and promiscuity that this group came to be labelled the "Happy Valley set". Their notorious goings-on, particularly the murder in 1941 of their leader, Joss Erroll, are regular topics of conversation in certain Kenyan social circles even today.

However the new colony could not escape the Great Depression. The early 1930s, just before Hemingway visited, saw the prices of maize, wheat, coffee and sisal fall drastically. Some of the avid party-goers of the 1920s fled home to Europe, and farms that had been just scraping by, such as Karen Blixen's Ngong coffee farm, failed. Only the most efficient farmers, who had diversified their crops, survived.

Hemingway's safari guide on his first trip, Philip Percival, was a successful farmer and also one of the greatest of the white hunters; and someone Hemingway was to admire for the rest of his life. His career as a professional hunter had begun with the Roosevelt safari, which persuaded many wealthy sportsmen from around the world to try their hand at big-game hunting. His burgeoning business was interrupted by the First World War, during which he worked for British intelligence, but he resumed hunting as soon as he returned to Africa, and quickly built his reputation. By the time he took Hemingway on safari, Percival was forty-nine and already had considerable experience in leading VIPs. His clients were often royalty or Hollywood stars like Gary Cooper, and of course the monied set, such as the Vanderbilts and George Eastman of Eastman Kodak; also the famed wildlife photographers Martin and Osa Johnson. His easy temper and calm authority made Percival the perfect white hunter for individualistic, challenging clients – of whom Hemingway was unquestionably one.

Ideally a safari client, now as then, should spend a significant amount of time with his or her guide/hunter before venturing out. Both parties then have a clear understanding of what they intend to accomplish. Although a guide/hunter acts as something of a mentor, the client is always in charge, always the final decision-maker. Nonetheless, the bond between client and guide/hunter often becomes close, with the amateur eager to gain the respect of the professional. Hemingway's affection for Percival, however, went deeper than a mere desire to impress. In *Green Hills of Africa* he pictured Percival as the gentle but commanding Pop – diplomatic and jovial, but also tough in the field. Percival insisted on certain unwritten rules about the taking of game. Though it is hard nowadays to make distinctions between 'necessary' and 'unnecessary'

The only other man Hemingway rated as highly as Philip Percival as a hunter was Bror 'Blix' Blixen, Karen Blixen's estranged husband.

killing, there were, on safari, honourable and dishonourable behaviours, brave and cowardly ways of encountering and killing animals. These ranged from the entirely acceptable daily kill 'for the pot' to the totally unacceptable shooting of prey from a moving motor vehicle. During Hemingway's first safari, the taking of trophies was part of the success of the client-guide relationship, but here too Percival had rules, and Hemingway noted that Pop "hated to have anything killed except what we were after, no killing on the side, no ornamental killing, no killing to kill, only when you wanted it more than you wanted not to kill it, only when getting it was necessary to his being first in his trade."[5] Hemingway wrote about Percival with unstinting praise throughout his life: a tone he seemed to find easier to adopt when describing men of action than fellow men of letters. In 1954, after his second safari, writing in *Look* magazine he called Percival simply "the finest man that I know."[6]

The only other man he rated as highly as a hunter was Bror Blixen, Karen Blixen's estranged husband. In a jaunty letter for *Esquire* magazine in 1934, Hemingway expressed his admiration for both men and their understated courage:

> There are two white hunters in Africa who not only have never had a client mauled – there are many such, but these two have never been mauled themselves; and there are very few of these. It is true that Philip Percival had a buffalo die with his head in the now ample Percival lap, and that Baron von Blixen, if there were any justice for elephants, would have been trampled to death at least twice. But the point is that they do not get mauled and that their clients get record heads, record tusks and super lions year after year . . .

> Both mask their phenomenal skill under a pose of nervous incapacity which serves as an effective insulation and cover for their truly great pride in the reserve of deadliness that they live by. Blix, who can shoot partridges flying with a .450 No. 2 Express rifle will say, "I use the hair trigger because my hand is always shaking so, what?" Or stopping a charging rhino at ten yards, remarking apologetically to his client who happened to have his rifle already started back to camp by the gun bearer, "I could not let him come forever, what?"[7]

Unlike Blixen, who was a notorious philanderer, and Denys Finch Hatton, who despite his famous romance with Karen Blixen remained a loner all his life, Percival was a happy family man who adored his wife and children. He had married his childhood sweetheart, Vivien Spark Smith, in 1909, and she proved to be an unusually strong and resourceful woman, well up to the rigours of life in Africa. It was Vivien who took over the management of their isolated Potha Hill Farm in Machakos, about two-and-a-half-hours' drive from Nairobi, during her husband's

Denys Finch Hatton and Karen Blixen had a complex intimacy in the 1920s. Both of them related hunting to seduction, believing that each pursuit sought possession of another creature's essence.

ever-increasing absences – as his safari career took off, Percival typically spent six to nine months of the year away from home – and who brought up their three children. Initially Potha Hill was an ostrich farm, but the trade in ostrich feathers declined with the rise in popularity of the motor car, since feather boas and the large plumes on hats were not practical for open-top motoring. During his 1909 safari, Roosevelt advised the couple that Potha was cattle country. So the Percivals switched the farm to beef, and by 1914 it was a going concern. The couple made a lasting impression on Roosevelt during his African tour: "I shall not soon forget seeing him one day, as he walked beside his twelve-ox team, cracking his whip, while in the big wagon sat pretty Mrs. Percival with a puppy and a little cheetah cub."[8]

On reaching Machakos, the Hemingways stayed with Vivien at Potha Hill while they waited for Percival, who was unable to join them until December 20. The delay provided time to adjust to the climate and altitude and to practise their shooting on gazelle and guinea fowl in the Kapiti Plain before the safari began. Hemingway made friends, too, with Alfred Vanderbilt, who was also waiting at the farm for *his* white hunter, Bror Blixen. Extremely wealthy, a successful lawyer, a world-class polo player and a man eager for trophies, Vanderbilt was typical of the Americans who could afford to enjoy a safari adventure in the 1930s. Hemingway had no trouble fitting in with plutocrats like Vanderbilt. He attracted famous people – kings, queens, Hollywood stars. Doubtless Vanderbilt was thrilled to know the bestselling writer.

✶   ✶   ✶

Like Hemingway, my visit to Machakos was a time of preparation – but for research rather than hunting.

Already, on the way to Machakos from Mombasa, along with Joerg Bondzio and Ernest Ombuya (our excellent cook) I had paid a visit to Ol Ngalau, the small but enchanting ranch owned by Joerg's father-in-law close to the shore of Lake Naivasha. Alwyn Smith and his German wife, Uta, have lived there for twenty-five years, and in that time the house has seen improvements that have made it spacious and breezy, with high ceilings and slowly circling fans. But despite having all the modern conveniences, it retains the charm of an earlier age: colonial furniture, some upholstered in bright chintz, and the lovely openness to the outdoors that is possible only in such warm climates. Although we were exhausted after a long day's travel, my ideas and opinions about

Left: Joerg Bondzio, of German and Italian extraction, is an experienced safari guide who has worked in both Kenya and Tanzania.

Opposite: A village faith healer performs a rather painful-looking procedure on a young woman in front of a crowd of curious Wakamba.

Hemingway were immediately pounced on as the household launched into an animated debate about the writer's first and second safaris. Joerg and Alwyn had recently returned from a reconnaissance trip around Kenya and Tanzania, digging up all kinds of Kenyan lore about where Hemingway had been and whom he had been with, the various tribes he had met and what he had thought of them. They were now bursting to share this research and their own ideas. All agreed that to look carefully at Hemingway in Africa would produce insights into the man and his works that could be gained in no other way.

Machakos, at the top of the Yatta Plateau, is the home of the Wakamba tribe. For Hemingway, the Wakamba were important people, and he grew close to them during his second safari. In *True at First Light*, he tells of his relationship with a Wakamba girl named Debba. Though parts of *True at First Light* are fiction, Debba was certainly real. But today, in contrast to Hemingway's day, the Wakamba have ceased hunting and gathering and taken up arable farming. Before this they tried

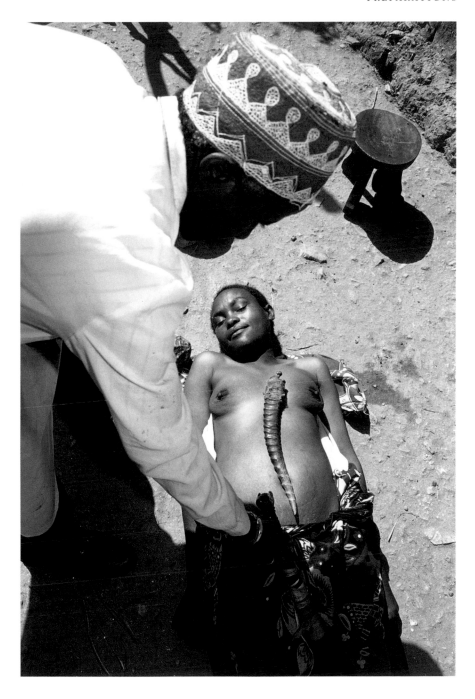

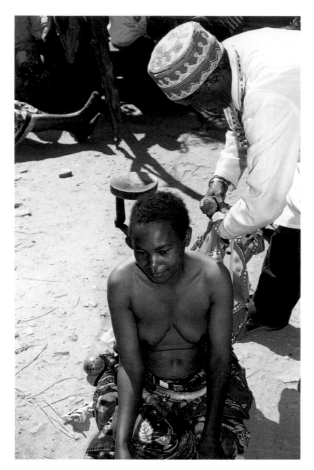

The healer wore a white cloak, and during the course of the half-hour treatment, he dug his knife into the woman's flesh and rubbed a dark powder into the wound.

cattle herding and farming, but they quickly proved failures at it; the serious erosion of the steep hills around Machakos makes good grazing nearly impossible to find. So nowadays most of the area is beautifully terraced, and vegetable and coffee growing dominates.

For my part, I had come to see a faith healer in the nearby village of Kathilani. I have long had an interest in the arcane practices of healers. The healer knew we were coming, but when we arrived, he was in the middle of performing a rather painful-looking procedure on a young woman in front of a crowd of curious Wakamba. I was unsure what sickness was being expunged from the woman as she lay, stripped to the waist, on the hot red earth. The healer wore a white cloak, and during the course of the half-hour treatment, he dug his knife into her flesh and rubbed a dark powder into the wound. This strange powder was only the final stage; before administering it, he had worked his way through a Thompson's gazelle horn, a warthog tusk, two emperor shells and a small calabash, and had even used a wildebeest whip. At length, the woman got up, apparently unharmed, though it was impossible to tell if the treatment had been effective.

I decided to take the plunge. I told the healer of the arthritis from which I have long suffered in my right groin and right shoulder. He agreed to perform a ritual for me similar to the one we had just witnessed. The knife wounds pierced my skin, though not deeply, and they certainly hurt. After rubbing the dark powder into my wounds, he gave me half a tumbler of a pungent grey fluid to drink. It tasted liked brewed garlic cloves – absolutely foul. And its effect was immediate: I sweated profusely and felt quite bilious on the journey back to the ranch as our Land Rover juddered over steep paths to regain the tarred road. The whole thing was in fact a risky and rather foolish medical experiment, for which I was later roundly scolded by a London doctor as he handed me a negative test report for HIV. But at the time I went through with it, I felt that it would help me in a small way to understand the relationship between the danger in Hemingway's life and the vitality in his writing.

CHAPTER 2

Hunting and Writing

. . . as we sat and leaned and felt sleep drain from us we were
as happy as hunters. Probably no one is as happy as hunters
with the always new, fresh, unknowing day ahead.

ERNEST HEMINGWAY
True at First Light[1]

On December 20 1933, after Percival had arrived in Machakos and the final preparations for supplies and transport had been checked and double-checked, Hemingway's safari party set off for the Tanganyikan border. Refusing to be diverted by the abundance of game all around, they arrived the next day at Namanga, checking their guns through customs. Then it was on to Arusha for one last night of luxury in a good hotel before finally reaching the Rift Valley, and moving up towards Lake Manyara and the Ngorongoro game reserve.

When our party reached Arusha, we met Diana Cordoza at the Kerr and Downey safari office. Her father was a good friend of Patrick Hemingway, Ernest's second son and Pauline's first, who worked in Africa as a safari guide in the 1950s and early 1960s. From what she could recollect, the colonials had liked Ernest Hemingway: "He was sort of a jovial guy. Hard-drinking of course, but fun. He was liked by the sporting set." By no means all of the opinions about him I would hear on my safari were as positive as this.

The Hemingway safari party set off for the Tanganyikan border on
December 20 1933.

I find that people are very opinionated about Hemingway and loathe to change their minds. In Britain he is often considered something of a bore, as well as overrated as a writer. In America, too, not everyone likes him, and those who do are not especially interested in his African experiences and writings. No one, however, disputes his heroic capacity for alcohol. All his women and the others around him tolerated his drinking, until it became one more element in the generally boorish, selfish behaviour that in the end characterized his intimate relationships. By then, outsiders put up with him because he was famous and paid the bills. He encouraged such hangers-on because he craved attention and adulation; he sought out those who could drink and carouse with him until dawn. But on safari drinking alcohol can be deadly. One or two drinks around the camp-fire at night are extremely pleasant; more than this dulls the requisite alertness. One can be attacked by thieves or wild animals, awake or asleep. Experienced travellers tend to sleep lightly on safari, never truly relaxing, never unaware of their immediate surroundings.

In the market in Arusha I bought an old walking stick and two bone-handled dolls, one male and one female, made to ward off animals and spirits. Later I acquired eight more Karuma dolls, quite rare and intricately carved. Made from wildebeest bone and rosewood, they contain *dawa* (ground medicinal substance), poured into a hole drilled in the bone and then sealed. My encounter with the faith healer at Machakos might not have been an unqualified success, but on safari I wanted all the luck and protection that was going! We ate at a roadside barbecue run by two Sunni Muslims, born in Kenya to Indian parents. Their stall has become one of the most popular eating places in Arusha, thanks to their chicken flavoured with garlic, chili and coconut cream. We had a long talk about India and Pakistan and the bloodshed that followed the 1947 partition, interrupted only by the *muezzin*'s call to prayer from the local mosque.

The next day, on our 190-kilometre journey to Lake Manyara, we stopped briefly to buy meat for the first two days of the safari. Obtaining fresh meat is a common safari challenge; on an earlier journey, following Burton, our party became violently ill from eating goat and beef sold by roadside vendors. In the past I have eaten zebra and crocodile, unusual but excellent, with a gamy taste like oxtail, and also eland and wildebeest, but this time we had to be content with beef biltong, salty, coriander spiced and sun dried. Unlike Hemingway, we did not have the option of shooting 'for the pot,' not only because it might have been illegal where we were going but also because we were carrying no guns, so as to avoid problems during our frequent border crossings. The Hemingway party made a clear distinction between hunting for the pot and hunting for trophies, although the eating of part of a trophy kill belongs in hunting rituals around the world even today. They did once claim to have eaten lion haunch marinated in sherry, but this sounds to me like bravado.

At about noon we reached Mto Wa Mbu ("Mosquito Village") – hot, dry, dusty, crowded and not at all the same little village I had first seen in 1988.

Back on the road, the biltong warded off hunger pangs; it is tough enough to keep one chewing for hours. At about noon we reached Mto Wa Mbu ("Mosquito Village") – hot, dry, dusty, crowded and not at all the same little village I had first seen in 1988. Then it was a small, quiet stopping-off point on the much-used red-sand road, a place where I bought the tiny, sweet sugar bananas known as plantains, and also an old, well-used Masai knife. From there we followed the winding red road to a point almost at the escarpment, where we got out of the Land Rovers and looked over Lake Manyara.

The incredible view I drank in was new to me, yet seemed somehow familiar. Then I remembered – from this very point Hemingway had first looked down into the Great Rift Valley. Although we had been following his route for some time, here was the moment when I felt that our two journeys were really starting to coincide. The night before, I had reread his description of the view in *Green Hills of Africa* and imagined it, and here it was laid out before my enchanted eyes, virtually unchanged since the 1930s:

> We had come down to the Rift Valley by a sandy red road across a high plateau, then up and down through orchard-bushed hills, around a slope of forest to the top of the rift wall where we could look down and see the plain, the heavy forest below the wall, and the long, dried-up edged shine of Lake Manyara rose-colored at one end with a half million tiny dots that were flamingoes. From there the road dropped steeply along the face of the wall, down into the forest, onto the flatness of the valley, through cultivated patches of green corn, bananas, and trees I did not know the names of, walled thick with forest, past a Hindu's trading store and many

The incredible view I drank in was new to me, yet seemed somehow familiar. Then I remembered – from this very point Hemingway had first looked down into the Great Rift Valley.

huts, over two bridges where clear, fast-flowing streams ran, through more forest, thinning now to open glades, and into a dusty turn-off that led into a deeply rutted, dust-filled track through bushes to the shade of M'utu-Umbu camp.

That night after dinner we heard the flamingoes flighting in the dark. It was like the sound the wings of ducks make as they go over before it is light, but slower, with a steady beat, and multiplied a thousand times.[2]

This is a fine example of Hemingway's talent for combining exact observation of details with sensitive appreciation of atmosphere. He had a near-photographic memory for landscape – his fourth and last wife, Mary Welsh, who accompanied him on his second safari, kept a diary of everything they saw together in case it might be useful to Ernest, only to find that he had no need of it because the information had all been filed in his head. Reading his description, we travel in glorious colour along that red road, above that pink lake, past the green corn and the clear stream to Hemingway's shady camp. We move in altitude and texture, down from the sandy plateau, through the forest, then out again to the lakeside. Finally Hemingway engages our aural senses by likening the flapping wings of flamingoes to a flight of ducks, a sound his readers can recognize. It is an intensely detailed yet economical mental tracking shot – no mere word picture – with which the writer moves us.

Credit here belongs in part to Hemingway's father, Dr Clarence E. ('Ed') Hemingway. He enrolled all his children in the Agassiz Club, an organization devoted to children's nature study through outdoors exploration. They were sent out, under the tutelage of an adult guide, to learn about the area's geology, flora and fauna, and to collect specimens for further investigation. They were encouraged to explain as accurately as possible and without recourse to guesswork or intuition what they saw in front of them. This strongly field-oriented science education was a significant part of Hemingway's training both as a naturalist and a writer. Accurate observation is the key to all his landscape descriptions: observation that he edited and sometimes mixed with emotion in the process of writing but which did not deviate from the facts.

Green Hills of Africa is the ultimate test of his passion for authenticity. Its foreword is explicit: "The writer has attempted to write an absolutely true book to see whether the shape of a country and the pattern of a month's action can, if truly presented, compete with a work of the imagination." Again, he shares his insistence on truth with René Maran, who cries out in his own preface to *Batouala* that France must listen to the facts about the mistreatment of black people in her colonies, and who insists that his picture of tribal life in colonial Africa is not polemic but objective truth. Hemingway's book lacks Maran's political agenda, but the Frenchman's claim that his novel is "entirely objective. It does not

Hemingway's father, Dr Clarence E. ('Ed') Hemingway, and his mother Grace enrolled their children in the Agassiz Club, an organization devoted to nature study through outdoors exploration. It sharpened Hemingway's nature writing.

even attempt explanation: it is a witness. It does not criticize, it registers"[3] – is pure Hemingway. But just as *Batouala* is more than a simple story about a tribal chief, so *Green Hills of Africa* is more than a straightforward chronicle of Hemingway's safari experience. It is also an exploration of his opinions on literature and an analysis of the pursuit and value of writing itself. He explains that it is through authenticity, the ability to put into accurate and sincere words the places, events and emotions one has experienced, that the writer can lay claim to a greater, more lasting significance than the rest of us. For the best writers, according to Hemingway, "have been there in the books and out of the books – and where we go, if we are any good, there you can go as we have been."[4]

✶   ✶   ✶

From Lake Manyara, our little party drove towards the dormant Oldeani volcano, intending to set up camp for the night in the Mongola district near Lake Eyasi and the enormous Ngorongoro Crater. Around here, in the Great Rift Valley, the Hemingway party began their hunt for lions. Judging from his descriptions, the landscape was little altered from his day. The lush land was still rich with game, and as I thought about Hemingway's love of wildlife and his lust for trophies, his desire for slaughter troubled me. For the twenty-first-century traveller schooled in the ethics of conservation, a hunter's keen enjoyment of the kill is hard to comprehend. What did killing mean to Hemingway? How did he explain the satisfaction it gave him?

At the end of *Green Hills*, he describes the kudu bull he shot after a long, arduous pursuit:

> I looked at him, big, long-legged, a smooth gray with the
> white stripes and the great, curling, sweeping horns, brown
> as walnut meats, and ivory pointed, at the big ears and the

The first safari. Hemingway's persistent desire to place himself in perilous situations or in the vicinity of danger – be it war or a bullfight or big-game hunting – was in the final analysis an effort to relive the intensity of existing at the edge.

great, lovely heavy-maned neck the white chevron between his eyes and the white of his muzzle and I stooped over and touched him to try to believe it. He was lying on the side where the bullet had gone in and there was not a mark on him and he smelled sweet and lovely like the breath of cattle and the odor of thyme after rain.[5]

The kudu's loveliness, its freshness and grace, engender no guilt. Yet elsewhere Hemingway shows a remarkable ability to empathize with animal suffering. Lying awake one night on the safari, he remembers the pain of recovering from a broken arm: "Alone with the pain in the night in the fifth week of not sleeping I thought suddenly how a bull elk must feel if you break a shoulder and he gets away and in that night I lay and felt it all, the whole thing as it would happen from the shock of the bullet to the end of the business."[6]

How can such lyrical appreciation of an animal and empathy with it co-exist with joy in killing it, with seeing it stone dead at one's feet? A long tradition of such oxymoronic 'naturalist hunters,' including Theodore Roosevelt and the Victorian explorer Frederick Selous, exists, and numerous explanations of this paradox have been given. The safari historian Kenneth Cameron argues:

> Death is at the centre of hunting and gives the sport seriousness, for death makes hunting an unnecessary and non-productive (that is, non-laboring) giving of death. Hunting's moral importance, too, springs from death, for it is only in the responsible acceptance of death-dealing that the hunter can claim respectability. The hunter cannot be indifferent to the death of the prey, or the hunter becomes morally contemptible; the hunter must will the death and will to accept the consequences of the death. Paradoxically, this seriousness has made the best hunters among the world's greatest lovers of animals, and it has made the act of hunting the essence of life for them.[7]

Both Karen Blixen and Denys Finch Hatton likened the thrill of the chase to seduction because hunting and seducing intend to possess the essence of another living being. Another writer with a vast experience of hunting, Bartle Bull, suggests that the desire to hunt is innate:

> The relationship between hunting and man's nature is inescapable. The more removed we become from nature, the

deeper our need for our lost natural environment. Hunting and fishing are the most intense form of man's integration, or re-integration, with nature. In the fullest sense, hunting may be considered a return to basics, for it reactivates man's dormant physical senses. For many hunters, some of whom today use a bow and arrow, a hunt is more satisfying and more fair to the extent that it is conducted on a more equal basis with the animal, a more primitive basis, relying on fewer people, less sophisticated equipment and less transport.[8]

However, Hemingway's own explanation relies on no philosophical or anthropological arguments. Instead, in *Green Hills*, he offers a very personal justification for his shooting:

> I did nothing that had not been done to me. I had been shot and I had been crippled and gotten away. I expected, always, to be killed by one thing or another and I, truly, did not mind that any more. Since I still loved to hunt I resolved that I would only shoot as long as I could kill cleanly and as soon as I lost that ability I would stop.[9]

He refers here to the wound he received on the Italian front during the First World War. Perhaps Hemingway's persistent desire to place himself in perilous situations or in the vicinity of danger – be it war or a bullfight or big-game hunting – was in the final analysis an effort to relive the intensity of existing at the edge.

René Maran certainly appreciated the notion, and once more *Batouala* provides the most relevant parallel. Maran too makes the point that proximity to death inevitably provides a heightened vitality, and the knowledge and fear of one's own death brings with it a sudden thrill, an awareness of the pulse of one's own heart: "What death, however great, could outweigh the swift movement, the joy of action, the intoxication of slaughter, in a word everything that makes life worth living?"[10] The kill is the defining moment in appreciating life.

Of course for Hemingway hunting was also wrapped up with courage and masculinity; bagging the trophies would somehow prove his virility. In his story "The Short Happy Life of Francis Macomber," he uses physical courage in the hunt as a shorthand for the personal qualities of the 'real' man. Again, Maran in his novel provides almost a commentary on Hemingway's own writing on the subject. While out hunting, Batouala thinks to himself:

> You hunt what you find. You hunt for the sake of hunting. It is the sport of the brave, the struggle of man against beast, of skill against brute force. There is plenty of danger, so hunting is the best training for war. Let who can prove his skill, his courage, his strength, and his endurance.[11]

As a newcomer to Kenya Karen Blixen was an eager hunter, but after a few years on her farm she hunted only enough to feed her companions.

For all this rationalization of why people hunt, it is a fact that many of the East African settlers who were keen hunters in their youth, later lost their hunger for the kill. As a newcomer to Kenya, Karen Blixen was an eager hunter, but after a few years on her farm she hunted only enough to feed her companions: "Before I took over the management of the farm, I had been keen on shooting and had been out on many safaris. But when I became a farmer I put away my rifles."[12] Similarly, by the late 1930s her ex-husband Bror Blixen became more interested in the photographic shoot than the shoot to kill: "These days I prefer to hunt with a camera. A good photograph demands more skill from the hunter, better nerves and more patience than a rifle shot."[13]

Hemingway himself shifted in attitude in the twenty years between his first and second safaris. He did shoot with guns on his second safari, but photography and watching wildlife were more important to him. In his 1951 article, "The Shot," he went so far as to declare: "The author of this article . . . admitting his guilt on all counts, believes that it is a sin to kill any non-dangerous game animal except for meat."[14] His later fiction too reveals a greater awareness of the ethical dilemma than his earlier novels, in which guilt is easily shrugged off. In *The Old Man and the Sea* (1952), the story of a man who is fishing not merely for a trophy but for his livelihood, Santiago's fierce connection to the natural world and respect for the marlin he is battling to land cause him to wonder: "If you love him, it is not a sin to kill him. Or is it more?"[15] This ambivalence, I believe, is at the core of Hemingway's experience of hunting in Africa.

The ethics of hunting are complex – witness the recent battle over fox hunting in Britain. Joerg, discussing Hemingway's attitude to killing over dinner at our camp in the Mongola district, at first delivered the conservationist's plea for hunting. Because humans have eliminated predators like the lynx and wolves (particularly in Europe), there is a need to keep down the numbers of the prolific breeders, such as deer, or they will do immense damage to forests and agricultural areas. Therefore, hunters must do a certain amount of culling, as natural predators once

did. Yet Joerg admitted to feeling, despite the nature of his livelihood, somewhat appalled by his own past activities in leading wealthy clients on trophy hunts for the "big five:" leopard, lion, rhino, buffalo and elephant. Still he had to acknowledge that hunting, even for trophies, exists for a legitimate reason: it creates revenue to maintain game parks and staff, and income for the poorest countries in the world such as Tanzania. The presence of legitimate hunters creates buffer zones around national parks and acts as a strong deterrent to poachers; without these hunting areas, poaching would continue unabated. A prime example was the ban on hunting in Kenya in 1977, after which Kenya lost nearly seventy per cent of its elephants to poachers in the following ten to fifteen years. Whereas in the same period Tanzania, in which hunting was still permitted, lost only forty-five per cent of its elephants. So it appears that professional hunting, to some extent at least, has a regulatory effect. Like Hemingway and other hunters of the early twentieth century, Joerg is ambivalent about killing animals.

I would never call myself a hunter. As a teenager in 1940s Ceylon I shot birds – duck, snipe, pigeons – with my father, and once killed a spotted deer high up in the jungle on our tea estate. Its death was so traumatic for me that the memory is still painfully sharp. I never killed an animal of any sort again.

At the end of Green Hills of Africa *Hemingway describes the kudu bull he shot after a long arduous pursuit. The kudu's loveliness, its freshness and grace, engender no guilt. Yet elsewhere Hemingway shows a remarkable ability to empathise with animal suffering.*

CHAPTER 3

The Fascination of Fear

Camping places fix themselves in your mind as if you had spent long periods of your life in them. You will remember a curve of your wagon track in the grass of the plain, like the features of a friend.

KAREN BLIXEN
Out of Africa[1]

Aware of the amount of ground we had to cover in just three weeks, we struck camp at 5.30 a.m., intending to push on south to Babati, near where the kudu hunt, which is the narrative focus of *Green Hills of Africa*, took place. As things turned out, though, we were sidetracked at a Hadza settlement near Lake Eyasi and invited to join their early-morning hunt.

The name Hadza is interesting and somewhat confusing. It is the anglicized form of Hasabe, the Swahili name for the Watindaiga tribe, the "people who live in the swamps" – in the old days, before European settlement, the tribe lived in the marshes around Lake Eyasi. Tom Msemo, the local village secretary, told me that Hasabe is a "clean" name; the tribe, unsurprisingly, grew to resent being referred to as the "swampy people."

Nowadays the Hadza number fewer than a thousand, and live in family groups of twenty to thirty members. They are similar in appearance to the bushmen of the Kalahari, their cheekbones perhaps not

The Hadza men living near Lake Eyasi are permitted to hunt in the traditional way with bows and arrows, without quotas or government restrictions.

Nowadays the Hadza number fewer than a thousand and live in family groups of twenty to thirty members.

Hadza men prepare their poisoned arrows, before setting off to hunt.

quite so high, and they speak a similar-sounding 'click' language. They are still hunter-gatherers, dependent on hunting for their survival. One of the young hunters we met wore a headband of a baboon tail. When we admired it, he sent a young boy to collect another headband, this one made almost entirely of the tail of a genet cat, which he modelled for us proudly. The Hadza men are permitted to hunt in the traditional way with bows and arrows, without quotas or government restrictions. For small game and birds, they use arrows with little hooks carved out of the arrowheads, and for bigger game they use poisoned arrows. During the rainy season, when food and water for the wild animals is plentiful, the game disperses and hunting becomes more difficult. Big game such as kudu or eland may be had only about once a month and must last the Hadza until their next kill. While we were there, food was scarce – the tribe seemed to live on old boiled eland skins – and a Spanish missionary, Father Miguel, arrived with a gift of a sack of maize; obviously we were not the only ones to notice the food shortage. Joerg gave a packet of digestive biscuits and two packets of the beef biltong we had purchased in Arusha, and later some sacks of ground maize. The Hadza's gratitude was effusive and touching.

We watched the men prepare their poisoned arrows, build a fire and light the small, L-shaped, stone pipe that the tribesmen use for their ritual *bhang* (marijuana) smoking. It must have been very strong marijuana, for as the pipe was passed around, there was much harsh, spasmodic coughing. When the smoking was over, it was time to set off, and we spent a unique hour and a half following the hunt. After only a few minutes' walk along the riverbed, a hunter just missed a dik-dik, then a guinea fowl roosting in a nearby tree. The arrow hit the guinea fowl's wing, and the bird flew off in a spray of feathers, while the arrow landed just a few yards from my feet. We returned to camp with the hunters as it began to rain. The women and children huddled in their grass-and-twig huts, but came out with the sun to perform a dance for us. Soon everyone joined in, clapping in rhythm.

The Hadza's ancestral lands are disappearing under constant pressure from all sides – agricultural corporations, tourists and professional hunters, and government resettlement programs. In the 1970s, the government gave the Hadza livestock, grain and tools for cultivation. But the effort to change the tribe failed, because they lacked agricultural know-how and the inclination to farm; as soon as the grain was finished, the tribe returned to its hunter-gatherer life. The government is still trying: attempts are being made to move the Hadza to Mongola Chini, an area on the southern shore of Lake Eyasi. The tribespeople are reluctant to go and refuse to give up smoking *bhang* in the morning. It is a case of the Africa of yesterday trying to survive in the Africa of today. One cannot help but feel that the present-day Hadza's time is limited.

After the hunt, we drove out across the dry, sandy flats of the southern shore of the lake. Hundreds of spoonbills waded in the shallows, sieving the water for food, and to the east a flock of pelicans stood in gangling elegance. A solitary yellow-billed stork ambled unconcerned across the front of our Land Rover. The noonday sun blazed overhead, but a cool breeze blowing off the lake made the temperature quite comfortable.

For lunch we had Russian sausage. I was amazed to encounter it in the middle of East Africa, until I reasoned that our cook had purchased it in Nairobi from a butcher catering for the tastes of those few German colonials still lingering in Tanzania. Later that day, I met Melanie Schmelling, whose husband had once employed Joerg. Now a widow with a small holding at the eastern tip of Lake Eyasi – cattle farming, some fishing, a camp-ground and eighty coconut trees – she is a reminder of the area's past when Tanzania was German East Africa. After Germany's defeat in the First World War, what could have been a great colonial development was confiscated and given to England under the name Tanganyika to 'protect.' Unlike more prosperous Kenya and Uganda, Tanganyika, later Tanzania, never received its due as a British protectorate. Even today, the British are not really loved in Tanzania.

Dinner was beef stew and maize on the cob – real man's stuff, giant cobs

The Ngorongoro Crater forms the summit of an enormous extinct volcano rising almost 3,000 metres from the hot dusty plains of the Serengeti.

with huge kernels cooked on an open fire. Monkeys chattered around the perimeter of the camp, never venturing too close to the giant acacia-wood fire blazing in the darkness. At the table with Joerg and me was Emanuele, the watchman from the Mzanzu tribe whom village secretary Tom Msemo had sent to guard us. He grinned at me, with a mammoth cob of maize in his hand and a bow and poison arrows resting by his side. Occasionally a Hadza or Mangati tribesman stopped by to trade, selling *bhang* pipes, bows with giraffe-sinew bowstrings, arrows and knives. I bought two knives, crudely made with animal skins and fur for sheaths. Above the camp, the acacias were in bloom, "like veins streaking across the sky," said Joerg. "They are the blood of Africa." The meal was a far cry from my usual dinner, yet one of the best I have ever eaten.

We were still headed for Babati and Hemingway's green hills. It is in an area populated by the Mangati tribe. "There's something you should know about the Mangati," Joerg remarked, chuckling at my suddenly

anxious expression. "I took a camping crew to central Tanzania back in 1988. We were driving through the Kizigo game reserve and I stopped near Babati, but the crew refused point-blank to pitch camp in the spot I'd chosen. When I asked why, all they would say was that the Mangati tribe were bad people. Well, that didn't seem like a good enough reason to me, so I insisted we stop, pitched my own small tent next to the Land Rover and went to bed. Next morning I realized that mine was the only tent that had been pitched. The rest of the crew had spent the entire night in the cabin of their transport lorry – eight people in that tiny cabin! It was only then that they told me, rather sheepishly, the story of the Mangati warriors who demonstrate their affection by cutting off a stranger's genitals and presenting them to their bride as a love token." I asked Joerg if perhaps we shouldn't consider camping somewhere other than the heart of the Mangati area the following night, but he just laughed and passed me some plantains.

The next morning, after a restless night troubled by a pair of scrapping serval cats, our first task was to clear the Mongola district barrier. We feared that we would not be allowed to leave, as there had been a cholera outbreak near our camp-site and the locals were forbidden to leave the area. Fortunately we got out with no need of a special permit. Considering the harrowing tales of disease – malaria, Ebola, sleeping sickness, bilharzia, AIDS – I have encountered in my African travels, it is odd that Hemingway never dwells on disease. Some of these diseases were not known during his time in Africa, or at least not by the names they have now, but even so there has always been a surfeit of virulent diseases in equatorial sub-Saharan Africa to lay low white explorers and visitors.

We drove on through a dry, hazeless morning, straight into the rising sun. To the northeast was Mount Oldeani, to the east the highlands of the

Mangati warriors are said to demonstrate their affection by cutting off a stranger's genitals and presenting them to their bride as a love token.

Ngorongoro Crater. The area we were crossing was a strange volcanic region, scrub littered with lumps of igneous rock. Beneath the Land Rover's wheels, a rough *maram* (lava) road stretched into the distance. The hours of bumping along it were punctuated by birdcalls – European rollers, francolins, guinea fowl, fiscal shrikes. Suddenly, from nowhere, a wildcat streaked across the road into a shallow ditch. At first glance it looked like a serval, but when we pulled over we could see it was a dark wildcat. Sightings of melanistic cats are very rare, and this was the first and quite possibly the last that either Joerg or I would ever see. Unfortunately the animal was too quick for my camera.

We continued to Karatu, going west, and then south on higher land. It was cooler now, more overcast, the road flanked by lush vegetation and fertile fields. The Mbulu tribespeople here wear much heavier clothing than the tribes of the lower, warmer lands around the soda lakes such as Lake Eyasi. Traces still remained of the heavy rains of five weeks before, puddles of brown water and rivulets here and there. We heard stories of people stranded by flooding for days. Picking our way through the Oldeani highlands and arriving at the hillside village of Mbulu just after noon, we were warned that the road we planned to take – down the escarpment to Magugu and on to Babati – was almost impassable, nothing but mud and slush. Only two or three days earlier, a Land Rover had apparently attempted the steep decline on the washed-out road, hit a deep rut and started a landslide which overturned the vehicle killing all three of its occupants. We decided to take a route further to the south-west via Dongobesh, even though it would double our journey to 140 kilometres. So it was down to Dongobesh, through much drier country, back on to rough, rutted, red roads, then up to Dareda and eventually to Babati.

By teatime we were at the foot of Mount Hanang in Mangati country, where the hot plains were full of cattle. Passing through a small village, we watched a Mangati craftsman make two brass bangles. From him we learned a little more about the tribe with the above-mentioned fearsome romantic practices. As well as being renowned for metal working, the Mangati were once great warriors. But in 1864 they were defeated by the Masai in a battle in the Ngorongoro Crater. Most of the remaining Mangati now live south of Lake Eyasi, and their hatred of the Masai lives

As well as being renowned for metal working, the Mangati were once great warriors. But in 1864 they were defeated by the Masai in a battle in the Ngorongoro Crater.

on. The very day before our visit, the newspapers had reported that Mangati men had killed twenty Masai in Kilosa, east of Mikomi National Park. The old tribal vendetta shows no sign of abating.

We passed a beautiful lake and a 16,000-hectare bean farm, started with Canadian aid, on the slopes of Mount Hanang. Soon we were south of Babati and on the road to Kibaya – well into Hemingway safari territory.

* * *

In *Green Hills of Africa*, Pauline Hemingway, Ernest agrees, is to have the first shot at a lion. After days of searching for a suitably impressive, heavy-maned beast, the moment arrives. The Hemingways' white hunter Percival points out the beautiful animal, and when it is within range, Pauline shoots with her Mannlicher. But she misses and Ernest's shot is the one that brings the lion down. However, the gun bearer, M'Cola, will have none of it. M'Cola is an older man with "slim, handsome legs with well-turned ankles on the style of Babe Ruth's," Hemingway notes, "and I remember how surprised I was the first time I saw him with the tunic off and noticed how old his upper body was."[2] M'Cola is absolutely devoted to Pauline; it is he who first calls her "Mama," and he sees the other hunters on the trip as "simply a lot of people who interfered and kept Mama from shooting things."[3] On this lion hunt, M'Cola insists that Pauline has made the kill, declaring: "Mama hit . . . Mama Piga. Piga Simba."[4] As a result, Pauline is swept along in a triumphal celebration, lifted into the air, caught up in the dancing and put in the awkward position of being hailed as a conquering hero when she knows she is not. Eventually, however, she succumbs to her fate as a brilliant huntswoman: "'You know, I feel as though I did shoot it,' P.O.M said . . . 'I don't believe I'd be able to stand it if I really had shot it. I'd be too proud. Isn't triumph marvellous?'"[5]

"Mama" has become "Poor Old Mama" (P.O.M.) in recognition of all that Pauline has to put up with in the way of uncivilized safari conditions and a frustrating husband. Although not a major character in *Green Hills*, nor a fully developed one, P.O.M. performs an important function. In the preface to the book, Hemingway advises the reader: "Any one not finding sufficient love interest is at liberty, while reading it, to insert whatever love interest he or she may have at the time." Obviously Hemingway's love interest was P.O.M., supportive wife and perfect safari companion. Tough in the field, she rejoices over her husband's trophies, commiserates and soothes when the day has not gone well, and never complains of tiredness or boredom. This is a loving couple whose one reported argument, over the discomfort of Pauline's boots, ends with the author's self-recriminations – he is "ashamed at having been a four-letter man about boots"[6] and anxious to make up. At the close of the book, when the triumphant Hemingway returns from the long kudu hunt, much of his pleasure in his success derives from being able to share it with his wife: "Then I was holding P.O.M. tight, she feeling very small inside the quilted bigness of the dressing gown, and we were saying things to each other."[7] His sketch of his second wife is drawn with much tenderness – though ultimately this marriage too would fail.

Hemingway's attitude towards women, as exhibited in his two African short stories, "The Snows of Kilimanjaro" and "The Short Happy Life of Francis Macomber," where they are seen as ruiners of men – differs sharply from that in *Green Hills of Africa* and *True at First Light*. In a sense, Africa was a gift that Hemingway eagerly presented to his wives: first to Pauline in the 1930s and then to Mary in the 1950s. Each woman accepted the offering – as had the wives of the nineteenth-century explorers Samuel Baker and Sir Richard Burton (the first of whom, Florence, travelled with Baker).

Pauline's own safari diary, which is unpublished, gives a more complex account of her part in the events recounted by her husband in *Green Hills*. The evenings were her favourite time, when the party relaxed after the day's exertions with glasses of whisky. She definitely enjoyed listening to Ernest and Percival tell stories round the fire. But the safari was not at all easy for a woman used to the comforts of city life. She was often bored, her diary reveals, for it was difficult to keep herself entertained while the men hunted and, when they were not hunting, talked about hunting.

In his book, Hemingway wrote about Pauline's shooting of a lion, but in his on-the-spot journalism he used his own experience of a lion hunt. His second "Tanganyika Letter" for *Esquire* magazine begins by arguing that the lion is not by nature Africa's most dangerous animal, since a lion,

> when you locate him in the morning after he has fed, will have only one idea if he sees a man, to get away into cover where the man will not trouble him. Until he is wounded, that lion will not be dangerous unless you come on him unexpectedly, so closely that you startle him, or unless he is on a kill and does not want to leave it.
>
> If you approach the lion in a motor car, the lion will not see you. His eyes can only distinguish the outline or silhouette of objects, and, because it is illegal to shoot from a motor car, this object means nothing to him. If anything, since the practice of shooting a zebra and dragging it on a rope behind the motor car as a bait for lion in order to take photographs, the motor car may seem a friendly object. For a man to shoot at a lion from the protection of a motor car, where the lion cannot even see what it is that is attacking him, is not only illegal but is a cowardly way to assassinate one of the finest of all game animals.
>
> But supposing, unexpectedly, as you are crossing the country, you see a lion and a lioness say one hundred yards from the car. They are under a thorn tree and one hundred yards behind them is a deep donga, or dry, reed-filled water course, that winds across the plain for perhaps ten miles and

gives perfect cover in the daytime to all the beasts of prey that follow the game herds.

You sight the lions from the car; you look the male over and decide he is shootable. You have never killed a lion. You are allowed to kill only two lions on the Serengeti and you want a lion with a full mane, as black as possible. The white hunter says quietly: "I believe I'd take him. We might beat him but he's a damned fine lion."

You look at the lion under the tree. He looks very close, very calm, very, very big and proudly beautiful. The lioness has flattened down on the yellow grass and is swinging her tail parallel to the ground.

"All right," says the white hunter.

You step out of the car from beside the driver on the side away from the lion, and the white hunter gets out on the same side from the seat behind you.

"Better sit down," he says. You both sit down and the car drives away. As the car starts to move off you have a very different feeling about lions than you have ever had when you saw them from the motor car.[8]

Hemingway was fascinated by fear all his life, and having had more than a taste of it in 1918 near the end of the First World War, he never under-estimated fear's significance: "In the war I was frightened, mechanically, enough times to understand fear and to realize its importance in life."[9] The question of a man's bravery or otherwise in the face of danger was a natural topic of conversation on the 1933–34 safari, and the subject of a hunter's losing his nerve would likely have been camp-fire talk between writer and hunter/guide as they swigged companionable aperitifs after along day in the field.

Hemingway used both the "very different feeling" he had personally experienced when stepping onto a level footing with a lion, as well as his criticisms of those who hunt game from a car, in writing "The Short Happy Life of Francis Macomber." This tale of a rich urbanite's safari experience is an examination of fear – the fierceness of its grip, its debilitating power and, eventually, the freedom and true manliness that result from controlling it.

He also used a real-life incident. It concerned J. H. Patterson, the ruthless railway engineer who killed the man-eating lions of Tsavo. The bare bones of what happened are that once upon a time Patterson took the Honourable Audley Blyth and his wife on safari, but returned from the bush only with Mrs Blyth, whom he later married. How her husband died is shrouded in mystery. Patterson's version was that Audley Blyth, maddened by fever, committed suicide and was hastily buried at a location he could not recall. There was another version, though, told by the African staff of the safari. They said that Patterson and Audley Blyth had quarrelled; that Mrs Blyth and Patterson had shared the same tent; and that she was with her husband in their tent when he was fatally shot.

Patterson died in 1947 in Los Angeles, without revealing any more. By then the story had been doing the rounds for decades. It surely triggered "The Short Happy Life of Francis Macomber," which Hemingway published in 1936. As Jeffrey Meyers writes in *Hemingway: Life into Art*,

> Hemingway, like everyone else in Kenya, must have been fascinated by the story of a beautiful wife who fell in love with a hunter and drove her husband to suicide. He heard this story from his white hunter Philip Percival (who later told the same version to Patrick Hemingway) while drinking around the evening camp-fire on his first African safari of 1934."[10]

In Hemingway's version, Macomber's fear grips him even before he

A Somali proverb says a brave man is always frightened three times by a lion; when he first sees his track, when he first hears him roar and when he first confronts him.

sees the lion that is to cause his shame. Lying at night in his tent next to his soundly asleep wife Margot, who does not love him, he hears a lion roar but has "no one to tell he was afraid, nor to be afraid with him, and, lying alone, he did not know the Somali proverb that says a brave man is always frightened three times by a lion; when he first sees his track, when he first hears him roar and when he first confronts him."[11] The following day, Macomber manages to shoot and hit the lion, despite rigid legs and trembling hands. But the animal is only wounded: "he turned his heavy head and swung away towards the cover of the trees as he heard a cracking crash and felt the slam of a .30-06 220-grain solid bullet that bit his flank and ripped in sudden hot scalding nausea through his stomach . . . Then [the gun] crashed again and he felt the blow as it hit his lower ribs and ripped on through."[12] Rather than simply acting as the trigger for Macomber's fear and the agent of his disgrace, the lion is a character in his own right. As it now gets ready to charge out of the cover where it has taken refuge, Hemingway's description conveys both understanding of the lion's pain and admiration for his bravery, and the terrible prospect the angry beast poses to an already terrified human:

> His flanks were wet and hot and flies were on the little
> opening the solid bullets had made in his tawny hide, and his
> big yellow eyes, narrowed with hate, looked straight ahead,
> only blinking when the pain came as he breathed, and his
> claws dug in the soft baked earth. All of him, pain, sickness,
> hatred and all of his remaining strength, was tightening into
> an absolute concentration for a rush.[13]

Delving this deeply into the lion's pain and emphasizing his nobility has a strange effect on the reader. Is having the courage to kill such a mighty animal really a test of true manhood? When the lion finally expires, his death is hateful: "the red-faced man worked the bolt on the short ugly rifle and aimed carefully as another blasting *carawong!* came from the muzzle, and the crawling, heavy, yellow bulk of the lion stiffened and the huge, mutilated head slid forward."[14] It is not just the dying lion which makes for a repulsive spectacle, but also the hunter and his gun.

The red-faced killer is not Macomber but his white hunter, Robert Wilson. For as soon as Macomber sees "the swishing rush in the grass,"[15] he makes a run for it, thereby flouting one of the chief unwritten laws of big-game hunting: you must be prepared to shoot yourself out of whatever trouble you have shot yourself into. Macomber's flight from the lion is the most public demonstration of cowardice imaginable. Apart from suffering a burning shame, he loses Wilson's respect and gains the sarcastic disdain of his wife Margot. That night he must lie awake and hear the sound of his wife slinking back into the tent from Wilson's bed. Yet the next morning he must breakfast with the man who has cuckolded him and who will now lead him back to the place of his humiliation in pursuit of buffalo.

The buffalo hunt changes everything. Seeing three buffaloes from the car, the two men jump out and in a moment, Macomber loses all his fear. Faced by the beasts, he feels nothing but "hatred of Wilson,"[16] and as a result he performs an excellent bit of shooting. Wilson acknowledges the loss of fear as a rite of passage: "He'd seen it in the war work the same way. More of a change than any loss of virginity. Fear gone like an operation. Something else grew in its place. Main thing a man had. Made him into a man. Women knew it too. No bloody fear."[17] Margot certainly notices the change and grows quiet, recognizing perhaps that the balance of power in her relationship with her husband has shifted.

Macomber does not get much time to enjoy his new-found manhood, however; his happy life is indeed short. Despite his good shooting, the first buffalo bull has only been wounded and has gone into the bush. There is, however, to be no replay of the lion episode. The new, brave, trigger-happy Macomber is determined to finish off the buffalo and is now fearless. "Instead of fear he had a feeling of definite elation."[18] As the bull charges out, Macomber stands stock still and fires repeatedly at its nose, as Wilson has instructed: "he could see the little wicked eyes and the head started to lower and he felt a sudden white-hot, blinding flash explode inside his head and that was all he ever felt." This explosion, its physical impact described in similar terms to the bullets felt by the lion, is the result of a shot fired by Margot. She had aimed "at the buffalo with the 6.5 Mannlicher as it seemed about to gore Macomber and had hit her husband about two inches up and a little to one side of the base of his skull."[19]

Did Margot intend to kill him? Hemingway states plainly that she shot at the buffalo, not at her husband, but it is easy to doubt her motivation, particularly if we see the white hunter, Robert Wilson, as the moral centre of the story. Wilson can be read as an example of a man free of women and of fear. He is the standard of true manhood: a moral guide, as well as a safari guide, for Francis Macomber. Wilson takes a dispassionate view of the Macombers' marital disharmony, enjoys Margot's body without being seduced by her, and is ultimately her judge. He holds Margot responsible for the death of her husband, believing that she fully appreciated the extent of the change in her husband, realized that she would no longer be able to behave as she chose towards him, and so took the first opportunity to get rid of him. "Why didn't you poison him?" Wilson asks. "That's what they do in England."[20]

A significant change made by Hemingway to the story of Patterson and the Blyths is that the fictional Macombers are Americans, not English aristocrats. Margot is the epitome of all that Wilson loathes about American wives, who are "the hardest in the world; the hardest, the cruellest, the most predatory and the most attractive and their men have softened or gone to pieces nervously as they have hardened."[21] Margot's physical beauty was modelled on Jane Mason, a young American socialite with whom Hemingway was involved in the mid-1930s and who, like Margot, was married to a rich husband whose chief romantic asset was his wealth. But there is little to suggest that Margot's *character* resembled Jane Mason's, and she appears to be too much of a caricature to be strongly based on any real woman. If we read Wilson as an example

The buffalo hunt changes everything in Hemingway's "The Short Happy Life of Francis Macomber." Macomber loses all his fear and performs an excellent bit of shooting.

of true manhood, then Margot is an example of woman as the enemy of man, abusing her husband while she has power and growing anxious when it seems she will lose this power. She is the archetypal Hemingway 'bitch,' and her hard beauty, scorn for her husband and willingness to cheat have often been cited as evidence that Hemingway's female characters fall into two camps – the submissive, saintly helpmeets and the emasculating vamps and bitches. By the time "The Short Happy Life of Francis Macomber" was written, this argument goes, the sensitivity Hemingway had shown to the female point of view in earlier stories such as "Hills Like White Elephants" or "Cat in the Rain" had dwindled into misogyny. Margot's beauty and sexuality are weapons she can use to break down her husband's self-confidence. Even if the shooting of Macomber is accidental, the picture holds: she drove him to his death.

Still, Wilson's is only one voice in the story, and recent critics, notably the feminist Nina Baym, have doubted his moral centrality. Baym points out that Margot has no need to shoot her husband if she wants to see him dead – the buffalo is going to kill him for her. Baym suggests that Wilson accuses Margot of murder so that he can blackmail her into keeping quiet about the fact that they chased the wounded buffalo in a car, an illegal act that would have cost a white hunter his licence.

Margot threatens Wilson's position, both as a professional hunter and as a role model of courageous masculinity. If Margot is going to appreciate big-game hunting as a true test of courage, she must first appreciate that it is a highly dangerous activity. Yet Hemingway suggests that Margot does not perceive the safari to be a true test of equals: "Just because you've chased some helpless animals in a motor car you talk like heroes."[22] In her view, man's technology awards him such a huge advantage over the game that the contest can never be fair. Stripped of his role as genuine protector, the white hunter is the arch-manipulator of false danger, engineering an adrenaline rush for his rich clients. Naturally, if Margot considers the safari experience a sham and is critical of the illegal use of the motor car, then Wilson will be anxious to silence her. The accidental death of her husband, which could be construed as murder, provides the ideal opportunity to keep her quiet.

It seems doubtful that Hemingway would endorse Margot's view of the safari; usually he is at pains to convey the true danger of big game.

But even if Baym's reading seems to contradict what we know about Hemingway, it shows that Hemingway's best fiction is more complex than that of his stereotyped public image. In his letters for *Esquire*, and to some extent in *Green Hills of Africa*, Hemingway cast himself as a confident, self-reliant hunter who knows how to handle a gun and a dangerous situation. He is respectful of fear, but never beaten by it; he has respect for big game, but he is there to kill it. Yet his fiction writing cuts through this journalistic PR to a deeper truth. "The Short Happy Life of Francis Macomber" is actually not a straightforward story about a triangle: manipulative bitch, weak husband and macho hunter. Rather, with its empathy for the lion, the story allows us to question the worthiness of the safari and its guide and to consider fear from many angles. It permitted Hemingway to address his own anxieties and insecurities in a way that his non-fiction could not. This is the aspect of the story that interests me most, as someone who is also fascinated by risk taking.

*   *   *

Today, the great attraction of so-called adventure travel, including safaris, shows that many people are still immensely concerned with their ability to conquer fear and are still willing, like the fictional Macombers, to invest money and leisure time in proving themselves fearless. In my own case, the quest to prove my courage began early and persisted until late in life. When I was eleven, at school in India, someone told me that if you could grab the queen from a beehive, the other bees would not harm you: that if you had the queen in your hand, the bees would swarm over your hand but not sting you. (I still believe this to be true.) One day just before supper, some classmates and I came across a large hive of bees in a tree. I told the others what I had been told. Of course they immediately dared me to shove my hand into the hole and grab the queen. I did – and was brutally stung.

In Green Hills of Africa *Hemingway wrote about his wife Pauline's shooting of a lion, but in his on-the-spot journalism he used his own experience of a lion hunt.*

Later I learned a great deal about fear from bobsledding – a sport that intrigued Hemingway too. Hurtling at 150 kilometres an hour down an icy chute in a 500-kilogram sled is dangerous. It is particularly so if the sled flips over – you must get out of the way of the heavy sled and let it go on ahead – or if it flies out of the run at high speed. Although the many corners of a chute are banked, sleds often fly out and can easily crash into trees or rocks or anything solid, almost always fatally for the driver and front men. In bobsledding, getting your mind into shape – overcoming fear – so that you can do your best to go down the run as fast as possible, is of paramount importance. Not surprisingly, it is also the best way to try to avoid injury.

On safari, I have gradually learned how to take risks with animals as a result of various close encounters. In Tanzania I was once sharing a small tent with my daughter when lions attacked our camp at night. We could hear a lion clawing the tent where our guides slept, followed by a scream. A lioness slunk around our own tent, seeming to respect our territory. Then she tripped over a guy wire and brushed against the canvas just a few centimetres from my face, obliterating the bright moonlight for a moment or two. I will never forget the putrid stench of her rain-soaked fur. My daughter and I kept as silent and still as the grave. There was no sound of any kind from the other tent, and we didn't know if the guides were alive or dead. We decided that if we were attacked, we would roll ourselves into balls to protect the front of our bodies: our eyes, throat and stomach. I had learned this defence from the Masai – for whom the conquering of fear is no hobby. In the end, the lions were satisfied with only our food boxes and water cans. We found these in the morning shredded and punctured with teeth marks.

But most of my close shaves on safari are the direct result of taking photographs. Peering through a lens can give one a false sense of security. Once, less than six metres away from a male leopard in a tree eating its impala kill, I stood up in an open Land Rover for a closer shot. The leopard's eyes were locked on mine. I was nervous but had the illusion of being in command. Yet it could have been all over for me in an instant. Another time, I approached a herd of buffalo on foot, camera at the ready, and saw a bull making his way through the herd towards me, lowering his head. Just a little warning, but enough. I moved slowly but purposefully back to the security of the Land Rover. If I had been injured, I would have had only myself to blame. But the closest I came to real danger was when shooting pictures of mating lions in the Serengeti for my first book. Sitting on the front fender of a Land Rover, I took a series

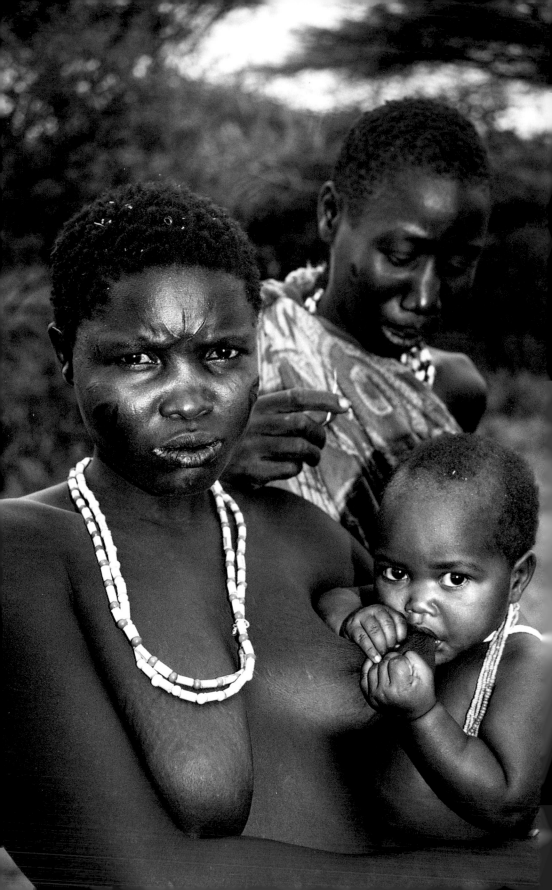

of terrific shots, culminating in a double-page spread of the male lion peeling himself off the lioness at the moment of climax. When the lions started to mate, I had shouted at my driver (who resisted at first) to drive slowly towards the pair until I was no more than two-and-a-half metres away. We disturbed them, and the male pulled away from the female; but I presumed the lions to be far more interested in each other than in me, and we were able to flee the scene. In retrospect, I suppose these shots required both calculation and nerve, and yet at the time I was not afraid but hugely excited. Partly because of the danger, but mainly because of the rare opportunity to take photographs. Photography – with its permanence, its shareability with others, and sometimes its dangers – continues to thrill me, as shooting with a gun once thrilled Hemingway.

Hadza woman and child. The name Hadza is interesting and somewhat confusing. It is the anglicized form of Hasabe, the Swahili name for the Watindaiga tribe, the "people who live in the swamps."

CHAPTER 4

Life on Safari

Its might is strangely weightless. At a distance, the mountain can seem ethereal. When the sun is low and the clouds light, the mountain with its white-shimmering cap seems at times to be floating in space. At such moments, Kilimanjaro seems almost supernatural in its beauty.

ROLF EDBERG
The Dream of Kilimanjaro[1]

By the end of December, Hemingway's life on safari had settled into an enjoyable rhythm. He and his party rose early and headed off in the morning cool to find their quarry. When the heat became unbearable, they returned to camp for lunch, followed by reading, writing and dozing in the shade. Then, in the late afternoon, they went off again in pursuit of game. The evenings were cosy – a bath, a change into pyjamas and mosquito boots, and a seriously carnivorous dinner – and of course boozy, as the whisky flowed along with the talk. Hemingway's capacity for alcohol had long been prodigious; and on safari it was monumental. Reading about his endless supply of bottles, I was reminded of Sir Richard Burton's provisioning of his caravan to cross East Africa seventy-five years before Hemingway's safari. Burton painstakingly detailed the tons of goods they had to carry and the numbers of porters necessary for the task. I could not help wondering which unfortunate lackeys slaved to carry all the cases of whisky knocked back by the Hemingways.

By the end of December 1933, Hemingway's life on safari had settled into an enjoyable rhythm.

That his writing eventually suffered from his drinking is not in doubt. *Green Hills of Africa* is the work of a writer in total control of his world and his words. But by the time of the events chronicled in *True at First Light*, on the second safari, the addled thinking and diminished awareness of the alcoholic are everywhere evident. Thus in *Green Hills*, the tolerant Pauline is described as gently puncturing the men's alcohol-inflated anecdotes around the camp-fire – and yet an ironic Hemingway is keenly aware of the interplay between the three of them as she speaks:

> "By God, you're brave as a little terrier." Pop and I had both been drinking, it seemed.
>
> "That's lovely," P.O.M. sat far back in her chair, holding her hands clasped around her mosquito boots. I looked at her, seeing her quilted blue robe in the firelight now, and the light on her black hair. "I love it when you all reach the little terrier stage. Then I know the war can't be far away. Were either of you gentlemen in the war by any chance?"
>
> "Were we not," said Pop. "A couple of the bravest bastards that ever lived and your husband's an extraordinary wing shot and an excellent tracker."[2]

The shooting on this first safari did indeed go well. Trophies were accumulating nicely. Hemingway told his *Esquire* readers:

> As far as bag goes, if anyone is interested, we have good heads of Eland, Waterbuck, Grant Robertsi and other gazelles. A fine roan antelope, two big leopard, and excellent, if not record, impala; also the limit all around on cheetah. They are much too nice an animal to shoot and I will never kill another.
>
> On the other hand we shot thirty-five hyena out of the lot that follow the wildebeeste migration to keep after the cows that are about to calve and wish we had ammunition to kill a hundred.[3]

Maybe Hemingway hated hyenas because of the way they hang around death. In "The Snows of Kilimanjaro," it is a hyena that can smell Harry's gangrenous leg.

Watching the hyenas' death throes was a source of amusement and delight for Hemingway and his gun bearer M'Cola. All of his powers of clear-eyed observation are to the fore in his description of hyenas in *Green Hills*, but his attitude entirely lacks the respect shown to nobler targets such as lions and kudus. About hyenas he is frankly sneering:

> . . . the pinnacle of hyenic humor, was the hyena, the classic hyena, that hit too far back while running, would circle madly, snapping and tearing at himself until he pulled his own intestines out, and then stood there, jerking them out and eating them with relish.
>
> *"Fisi,"* M'Cola would say and shake his head in delighted sorrow at there being such an awful beast. Fisi, the hyena, hermaphroditic, self-eating devourer of the dead, trailer of calving cows, ham-stringer, potential biter-off of your face at night while you slept, sad yowler, camp-follower, stinking, foul, with jaws that crack the bones the lion leaves, belly

dragging, loping away on the brown plain, looking back, mongrel dog-smart in the face; whack from the little Mannlicher and then the horrid circle starting. *"Fisi,"* M'Cola laughed, ashamed of him, shaking his bald black head. *"Fisi.* Eats himself. *Fisi."*[4]

Why Hemingway had it in for hyenas so violently is a bit of a mystery. While the hyena is never likely to feature in a list of the world's top ten most-appealing creatures, its ugliness should not merit its vicious slaughter. His relish in annihilating hyenas is grotesque – like a small boy gleefully pulling the legs off a spider. He and Thompson, his *Green Hills* hunting companion, kept a tally of the hyenas they disposed of, meant as a joking counterpoint to the really important business of which man bagged the best 'big five' trophies. Maybe Hemingway hated hyenas because of the way they hang around death. In "The Snows of Kilimanjaro," it is a hyena that can smell Harry's gangrenous leg; and a hyena's strange but somehow human cry that disturbs Harry's wife, Helen, as she wakes on the morning of his death.

*　*　*

Driving south from Babati, we were approaching two camps used by Hemingway near Kolo and Kondoa, from where he hunted kudu, buffalo, impala, Thompson's gazelle and rhinoceros. Here and there on the more thickly forested slopes to either side of the red-earth road were plantain plantations, between them mango groves and fields of castor-oil plants. We saw a handwritten notice tied to a *mwule* tree offering for sale small coffee bushes. The Land Rovers climbed up into *miombo* – thicker savannah woodlands.

Arab influence was obvious here. One can usually spot an old caravan route used by Arab slave traders from the date palms that line the road, which have grown from the date pits discarded by the merchants on the way into and out of the interior. For a while I wondered if we might be travelling the old slave route from the coast through Dodoma, possibly all the way up to Devora – but this time going in the opposite direction to my earlier journeys in the footsteps of the explorers Burton and Speke. In fact it was a different one. Several old slave routes are still used in Tanzania because they remain the quickest way for people and goods to move across most of the undeveloped reaches of East Africa. Besides, the routes are rich in tradition and history, grooved by the feet of the tribal people betrayed by their own chiefs to the Arab slavers, by the feet of the chiefs and slavers themselves, and by those European missionaries determined to win Africa for the Christian God, and European explorers eager to win her for science and territorial gain. Hemingway, whether he knew it or not, was following in all of their footsteps, in his personal quest to win Africa for himself.

Near Kondoa, after a stiff climb on foot along a narrow, irregular footpath, we reached some caves in the *kopjes* (rock outcroppings) well known for their prehistoric paintings. Louis and Mary Leakey first visited the site in 1935, and in 1951 they returned, with their young sons in tow (including Richard), for a thorough investigation. The Leakeys put the age of the surviving paintings, which are located on the side and underside of rock overhangs, at a few thousand years old, though colouring materials scientifically dated as 29,000 years old have been found in the area. Paskal Lububa, a curator from the antiquities department in Kolo, told us that the style of the paintings corresponds with the Aurignacian paintings from southwest France. The painters mixed their pigment with fig-tree sap and mammoth fat to create a distinctive red. Their ancient depictions of dancing, wildlife and hunting ceremonies are still charming, despite the depredations of time, weather and human defacement since 1951. (One can see them as they once looked in Mary Leakey's copies of the rock paintings, which her daughter-in-law discovered in a tin trunk and published in 1983 as *Africa's Vanishing Art: The Rock Paintings of Tanzania*.)

When we emerged from the caves and I stood on a high bluff, I could look down on the land where Hemingway had hunted. Time – thousands of years of history – seemed to telescope: the rock paintings, the slavers, the nineteenth-century explorers, the missionaries, Hemingway's safari and our present-day researches, all seemed, at least passingly, to overlap.

*   *   *

To judge by his writing about his first safari, Hemingway fell head over heels for Africa. The romantic metaphor is the one he himself employed in *Green Hills of Africa*:

> Now, looking out the tunnel of trees over the ravine at the sky with white clouds moving across in the wind, I loved the country so that I was happy as you are after you have been with a woman that you really love, when, empty, you feel it welling up again and there it is and you can never have it all and yet what there is, now, you can have, and you want more and more, to have, and be, and live in, to possess now again for always, for that long, sudden-ended always; making time stand still, sometimes so very still that afterwards you wait to hear it move, and it is slow in starting. But you are not alone, because if you have ever really loved her happy and untragic, she loves you always; no matter whom she loves nor where she goes she loves you more. So if you have loved some woman and some country you are very fortunate and, if you die afterwards it makes no difference.[5]

The passage may be rather purple and overwrought, but then love letters often are. As a declaration of belief in the permanence of romantic

Near Kondoa, after a stiff climb on foot along a narrow, irregular footpath, we reached some caves in the kopjes *(rock outcroppings) well known for their prehistoric paintings.*

love, it is overweening. Yet it surely conveys Hemingway's passion for East Africa. The mammoth convoluted first sentence (especially by Hemingway's famously terse and transparent standards) sweeps us along on a tide of insatiable desire for an Africa imagined as the ideal woman, the woman you will never tire of and who will always offer you her devotion.

But despite his overwhelming joy in the landscape of Tanganyika, all was not rosy for Hemingway. He had suffered from diarrhoea since the start of the safari. By mid-January, he was in too much pain to continue hunting and his condition was serious enough to need hospital treatment; any beneficial effects of the chlorine salts Percival had prescribed had been completely undone by alcohol. It was obvious he had amoebic dysentery. Percival decided that his client must go to Arusha, and he sent the driver, Ben Fourie, on the 160-kilometre journey to the nearest telegraph station to wire for an aeroplane to reach their camp on the following day. But the plane was delayed, and Hemingway was forced to wait. Unpleasant though it must have been, the experience was not wasted. For this episode undoubtedly fed into the writing of "The Snows of Kilimanjaro." When they finally took off, the pilot flew his invalid passenger past the mountain's great snowy peak on the way to Arusha, just as Hemingway would later describe in the finale of his great story. For him, however, unlike his dying character Harry, ahead lay recovery.

✳ ✳ ✳

After Kondoa, we took a sharp turn to the east on the dusty road across the Masai Steppe to Kibaya, Kiberashi and thence to Handeni, about 240 kilometres distant and a further Hemingway camping spot. Soon after the turn, we saw some Warangi youths bathing in a sunlit stream, splashing and play-fighting, their deep-black skin glittering with droplets of water in the tangerine evening light. Then we drove on through dry scrub-

Warangi youths bathing in a sunlit stream, splashing and play-fighting, their deep-black skin glittering with droplets of water in the tangerine evening light.

land, interspersed with maize plantations, baobab trees and dry riverbeds
rutted by the recent rains – with a restful vision of hills far to the south.
There were also cattle, part of the enormous herds still kept in the area
by the Mangati; we passed the occasional solitary Mangati tribesman
carrying his spear.

The odd Christian mission signboard notwithstanding, this is a
predominantly Muslim area, as it was during Hemingway's safari. The
second gun bearer mentioned in *Green Hills*, after the Pauline-loving,
hyena-mocking M'Cola, was Charo, a Muslim. He was "short, very
serious and highly religious. All Ramadan he never swallowed his saliva
until sunset and when the sun was almost down I'd see him watching
nervously." Hemingway adds:

> The Mohammedan religion was very fashionable and all the
> higher social grades among the boys were Mohammedans.
> It was something that gave caste, something to believe
> in, something fashionable and god-giving to suffer a little
> for each year, something that made you superior to other
> people, something that gave you more complicated habits of
> eating, something that I understood and M'Cola did not".[6]

Today Islam is even more widespread; more than a third of Tanzania's
population of 33 million are Muslims. It is no longer restricted mainly to
the coast, but has spread inland.

By 5.30 p.m. we were tired, dirty and hungry: time to find a camp-site.
Ten minutes went by in chasing two chickens we had bought for about
three thousand shillings – a few dollars. They put up a good struggle;
but dinner that night was still destined to be chicken curry, with fried
plantains and *ugali*, a mash made of millet, the Tanzanian equivalent of
bread. Continuing eastwards for a bit longer, we pitched camp in what we
thought was a pleasant, secluded spot, well into the *miombo* away from

Enormous herds of cattle are still kept on the Masai Steppe by the Mangati.

the dirt road. We set up our usual two fires, one for cooking and one for warmth around the tents, and settled down. As we were enjoying our beer, we heard the sound of cattle bells coming closer and snatches of surprised chatter as villagers, some with cattle, walked right by the tent fire and on into the pitch-black *miombo*. Even as late as 8 p.m. they were still trudging past the fire. Everyone was friendly – "*Jumbo, habari, poleya safari*" ("Sorry for your long journey") – to which we replied, "*Asante. Pole kusumbua, wewe*" ("Sorry for causing you trouble"). Inadvertently, we had put our tent fire slap in the middle of a village thoroughfare.

But it was a lovely place anyway. Curiously, and happily, because there were no mosquitoes we could simply enjoy the crackle of the fire and the conversation as dinner was cooked. Joerg was studying his maps, calculating distances, compiling statistics, checking and double-checking our route – 406 kilometres via Handeni to Tanga on the coast. There we would stop, before crossing back into Kenya and driving along the coast to Mombasa. Eventually he was done, and dinner was ready.

Then, as we relaxed by the fire, stomachs rumbling pleasantly, waving hello to the occasional passing villager, I raised the possibility of flying around Kilimanjaro, to see the great mountain – and Leopard Point – close up, like Hemingway. And this inevitably set off some reminiscences from Joerg about *climbing* the mountain. He told me a strange story from personal experience, about an American socialite known for her mountain-climbing adventures, and some gold crosses. It is a tale that might well have appealed to Hemingway with its slightly lurid combination of wealth, daring and obsession.

"I was climbing Kilimanjaro in 1993," said Joerg, "and Sandy Pittman happened to be scaling the mountain at the same time, guided by the American mountaineer Scott Fischer. On the way up, she told me that it was her great ambition to climb the highest mountain on each of the seven continents: the seven summits. She had already climbed Mount Elbrus in Russia, Aconcagua in South America, Mount McKinley in North America and now Mount Kilimanjaro and was soon heading for Everest, her fifth peak." (Three years later, Pittman would successfully climb Everest, again led by Fischer, but he and seven others would die during the descent, though she would survive.)

While we were at the Horombo hut, exactly half-way down the mountain at 3700 metres, Sandy told me that she had commissioned a goldsmith in Arizona to make her fourteen gold crosses. Seven were for her when she had climbed each of the seven peaks, and seven were for the mountains themselves. She would place one on the summit of each successfully scaled mountain. The cross weighed about three hundred grams and must have cost at least two thousand dollars – an extraordinarily expensive gesture. She told me exactly where she had placed her gold cross on Kilimanjaro – in her wide-necked water bottle, just underneath a rock in a small crevice two metres from the Uhuru peak, the mountain's highest point. She had tied an orange ribbon around the water bottle – to make it easy to find, because she wanted someone to find it. Inside the bottle was a note saying that the gold cross was for the person who found it, and that she wanted this person to contact her in America. Then she asked me to scale the mountain again and find the cross for myself.

As it turned out, my next climb up Kilimanjaro was only ten days later, so I had a pretty good chance of finding the gold cross. I was keen to find it, not just for its value, but also for the experience and because Sandy had said she would like it to be me who found it. However, as fate would have it, by the time my American client and I reached Gilman's Point, just 150 metres below the Uhuru summit, he was too exhausted to continue. As the lead guide, I felt I couldn't continue to the top and had to get the party back to the bottom. My next climb up Kilimanjaro was six months later. This time, my client and I did make it to the summit, but neither the water bottle nor the gold cross was anywhere to be seen. No one has ever contacted Sandy about it, so the whereabouts of the cross remain a mystery.

☆ ☆ ☆

Hemingway, surprisingly and perhaps significantly, never climbed Kilimanjaro, only flew past it on his way to Arusha, where he did not stay long. He moved to Nairobi in order to receive regular emetine injections, though he neglected to inform his wife or Percival of his change of plan. Soon he was well enough to get out into Nairobi society, to start knocking back the booze again, and to write a typically facetious account of his distress for *Esquire* magazine:

> According to Dr Anderson the difficulty about a.d. [amoebic dysentery] is to diagnose it. My own diagnosis was certainly faulty. Leaning against a tree two days ago shooting flighting sand-grouse as they came into a water hole near camp after ten days of what Dr Anderson says was a.d. all the time, I became convinced that though an unbeliever I had been chosen as the one to bear our Lord Buddha when he should be born again on earth. While flattered at this, and wondering how much Buddha at that age would resemble Gertrude Stein, I found the imminence of the event made it difficult to take high incoming birds and finally compromised by reclining against the tree and only accepting crossing shots. This, the coming-of-Buddha symptom, Dr Anderson describes as prolapsus.
>
> Anyway, no matter how you get it, it is very easily cured.

Hemingway, surprisingly and perhaps significantly, never climbed Kilimanjaro, only flew past it on his way to Arusha, like Harry in "The Snows of Kilimanjaro."

You feel the good effects of the emetine within six hours and the remedy, continued, kills the amoeba the way quinine kills the malarial parasite. Three days from now I will fly back to join the outfit in the country to the south of Ngorongoro where we are going to hunt greater Kudu. But, as [already] stated, there is no typewriter; they won't let you drink with this; and if the reader finds this letter more dysenteric than the usual flow, lay it to the combination of circumstances.[7]

If Hemingway had known about the *mele mele* tree, he might have avoided the worst effects of amoebic dysentery. When one of our party had a stomach ache, our Tanzanian guide Andrea Kinyozi stripped some bark off a *mele mele* with an axe. Joerg interviewed him in Swahili, and then translated for my benefit, as the bark was boiled down to a dark brown liquid. Swallowed, it cures diarrhoea, constipation, flatulence and even dysentery: apparently it is a complete stomach cure, very similar

If Hemingway had known about the mele mele *tree, he might have avoided the worst effects of amoebic dysentery. Its bark is a cure-all for stomach trouble.*

to the effects of the liquid formed by boiling up the hard, dried, black flowers and berries of the *beli* tree in Sri Lanka.

While recuperating in Nairobi, Hemingway came to know Bror Blixen, and the two men hit it off – which is not surprising given their similar appetites for hunting, womanizing and life in general, plus of course Hemingway's admiration for Blixen's prowess with a gun. They soon planned an end-of-safari fishing trip together with Alfred Vanderbilt, whom Hemingway had met at Percival's farm in Machakos. 'Blix' also introduced Hemingway to his aerial game scout, Beryl Markham.

She was an extraordinary Englishwoman, who had lived dangerously in Africa with the kind of brio and courage that Hemingway sought for himself. Brought up in the bush, Markham could throw a spear as well as her African friends, had an intuitive way with horse breeding and racing, and then picked up solo flying, later making the first solo trans-Atlantic flight from east to west – on top of which she was the quintessential long-legged, blond bombshell. She had affairs with Prince Henry (third son of King George V), with Denys Finch Hatton and with Bror Blixen, to name but a few. But always she remained self-contained and fiercely independent.

Markham could hardly be described as Hemingway's ideal woman. Her independence and casual attitude towards sex would have disqualified her as a helpmeet, and her astonishing sporting and flying ability would have been threatening to him. After Nairobi, Markham and Hemingway met only once more, in Paris, when she flew Bror Blixen across north Africa to Europe some time between 1936 and 1938 (the date of the flight is disputed). Blixen's own surprise and pleasure at bumping into Ernest in Paris is clear from *Bror Blixen: The Africa Letters*. Having landed and left his suitcases in a nearby shed, Blixen comments:

> There was another man in the shed fiddling with his luggage, and as he was leaving I thought I recognized his gait – however, it could not very well be that person because he

was in Spain. Yet who else walked in that particular way, with those long arms like a gorilla's?

"Ernest!" I shouted, and sure enough, it was Ernest Hemingway, unshaven and dirty, but him, without a doubt.

"What are you doing here?"

"I could ask the same." I from Africa and he from the Spanish Civil War.[8]

They spent the night at the Ritz, and the next morning Hemingway, Blixen and Markham renewed their former contact while doing a little sight-seeing, before the twosome flew on to London.

Between Hemingway and Beryl Markham there was therefore barely more than an acquaintance. Yet Hemingway would later play a surprising posthumous role in Markham's literary reputation. Her book about Africa, *West with the Night*, is now considered a classic account of life in colonial Kenya, almost on a par with Karen Blixen's *Out of Africa*; but its path to

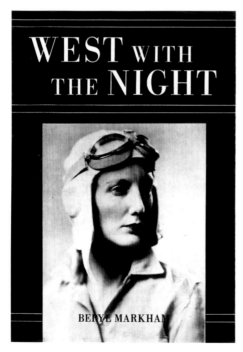

Hemingway thought so highly of Beryl Markham's West with the Night *that he told his Scribner editor Maxwell Perkins that "she has written so well, and marvelously well, that I was completely ashamed of myself as a writer . . . This girl . . . can write rings around all of us who consider ourselves writers."*

critical acclaim was not smooth. It sold well when it appeared in 1942, despite whisperings that the book was an implausible achievement from this far-from-bookish woman and must have been partly the work of her then-husband, the American editor Raoul Schumacher, helped also by her friend the French writer Antoine de Saint-Exupéry (*Night Flight* and *Wind, Sand and Stars*). But this was wartime; the subject of Markham's book was not topical, and its success was temporary. Within a relatively few years, *West with the Night* had fallen out of print, and its author's remarkable life story and magical evocation of pioneering Kenya were all but forgotten.

Hemingway thought so highly of the book that he told his Scribner editor Maxwell Perkins that "she has written so well, and marvelously well, that I was completely ashamed of myself as a writer . . . This girl . . . can write rings around all of us who consider ourselves writers." His humility was however tempered by an acerbic personal remark, that Markham was known to be "very unpleasant and we might even say a high-grade bitch . . . She omits some very fantastic stuff which would destroy much of the character of the heroine; but what is that anyhow in writing?"[9] Since Hemingway only knew Markham briefly in Nairobi, this sounds more like calumny than truth, and it seems likely he was influenced by the undoubted Nairobi gossip, especially about her sexual promiscuity. She may even have rejected his sexual advances, according to Markham's biographer Mary S. Lovell on the basis of one old rumour.

At any rate, Hemingway's literary respect turned out to be extremely influential in rehabilitating Markham's book. In the 1980s, his letter to Perkins led directly to another publisher's rescue of *West with the Night* from literary oblivion. The second time around, in a feminist age, there was greater critical acclaim than when the book first appeared. Happily Beryl Markham was still alive – and again living in Kenya – to enjoy the eventual triumph of her extraordinary tale.

CHAPTER 5

Art versus Sport

*"You really like to do this, what you do now, this silliness of
  [hunting] kudu?"*
"Just as much as I like to be in the Prado."
"One is not better than the other?"
"One is as necessary as the other."

ERNEST HEMINGWAY
Green Hills of Africa[1]

Our camp on the way to Handeni in the middle of the village path may
have been blissfully free of mosquitoes, but it had more than its share
of bees. At first light they came after us as we stirred from our tents.
The swarm was very disconcerting, buzzing around my chest, neck and
head while I washed, apparently attracted by the moisture. My boyhood
bravado with bees at school in India has long since been replaced by
caution, and I resisted the temptation to swat them as we packed up
camp. If you kill a bee, it is said, the swarm 'knows' and attacks. In
Africa, bees are responsible for more deaths than any creature except
the hippo.

Joerg told me he once had to treat an Italian client who had been
badly stung. The man had been hunting *sitatunga*, a kind of web-footed
antelope, in the swampland of the River Moyowosi in western Tanzania.
To help the search, a tracker climbed a huge fig tree. At the top he sighted
a dark cloud moving towards him. With a scream he hurled himself some

*In the small town of Sikwakwa in Tanzania a garrulous man with six fingers
on one hand regaled passers-by with local folk tales and superstitions.*

twenty feet to the ground, and the entire group fled, followed by the cloud. The Italian, though warned not to swat the bees, could not resist and started slapping at his face as he ran through the swamp, and killed a bee. Immediately the swarm swooped on him. In panic, he cried out for help and began throwing his equipment into the swamp. Joerg and his boss, Raoul Ramoni, ran back, but all they could do was to grab the victim's hair and shove his face into the mud, pulling it out every thirty seconds for air. In the process, they themselves were stung about eight times and the Italian at least thirty times. Only Joerg's quick injection of hydrocortisone saved him from certain death.

Much of our drive was now through wide-open hunting country alive with game. In the small town of Sikwakwa we bought some Mbulu work knives, made with a half-axe handle and used for cutting cane, maize and wood. The vendor was a garrulous man with six fingers on one hand, someone easily imaginable as a bit part in a Hemingway story, proudly showing off his special hand and regaling his customers and passers-by with local folk tales and superstitions. He claimed that in the Pare Mountains, east of Arusha and south of Kilimanjaro, there is a sheer rock face called Jiwa La Watoto, meaning "rock of the children," which drops one hundred metres from a narrow ledge at the top. If a local child is born with a sixth finger or if its teeth emerge first in the lower jaw, after dark the parents abandon the infant on the ledge. "The child is left to its fate," said the knife vendor. "Either it falls off the cliff to its death, or it falls on to the other side away from the fatal drop" – rarely does it stay steady on the ledge until morning. Babies who survive are usually picked up and adopted by strangers. When we told the man that in the western world a sixth finger is considered lucky, he was very pleased with the information and laughingly let us photograph him.

Several dik-diks crossed the road, then we spotted bush buck, guinea

Most people in Handeni were wearing shabby western clothes, except for some women in traditional kangas. *Hemingway would hardly recognize the place today, judging from what he wrote in* Green Hills of Africa.

fowl, African partridges, knob-billed ducks and comb ducks – the last of which, though fairly numerous in the wetlands, strangely are seldom seen. We saw no impala because the *miombo* was quite thick and green, thanks to the recent rains. Away from the road, invisible to us, there must have been many plain-coloured antelope, as well as buffalo and kudu. But no longer any giraffes, mainly because they are such easy quarry for lions and leopards – and poachers.

Just after Kiberashi, we turned off the road for lunch, stopping at one of the few places with shade trees. The haunting jangle of cattle bells in the distance reminded me of Burton's favourite sound: camel bells. Back on the road, at a small village we bought a strange, small, dried fish, known locally as *berege*, with a disturbing resemblance to a piranha fish. Its smell reminded me of maldive fish, often used in curries in India and Sri Lanka.

By four in the afternoon, we were in Handeni, a sleepy, dirty town. Most people were wearing shabby western clothes, except for some women in traditional *kangas* – no sign of Masai or Mangati tribesmen here. Children poured out of school in their blue-and-white uniforms and raced up for a closer look at our dusty Land Rovers. Sitting by the roadside, beneath a line of telephone poles and wires, I could see agricultural settlement in the surrounding plain. Seventy years ago, when Hemingway camped near Handeni, this plain was probably inhabited only by game. He would hardly recognize the place today, judging from what he wrote in *Green Hills of Africa*.

Twenty-seven per cent of Tanzania is devoted to game parks, the largest percentage in any country. If the herds of wild animals are to survive, it will only be because of the game park policy. In Kenya, for decades there has been political debate about whether some of the game parks should be given to the people for building houses. In Tanzania, too, the pressure on the politicians is definitely mounting and seemed to be more intense on this safari than during my visit five years before. When huge tracts of the country are set aside for hunters, most of them foreign, then Tanzanians

Sable antelope, east of Handeni, where Hemingway's white hunter Philip Percival established a new camp for the Hemingway party in early 1934.

are, in a sense, being robbed of their own land. Though large amounts of foreign cash and foreign aid are attracted by the parks, ordinary Tanzanians feel they derive little benefit from the money. Complicated though the economic issue has become, the people undoubtedly have a legitimate argument. I doubt if Tanzania's game parks can survive in their present form.

East of Handeni, the *miombo* is being cleared and cultivated for small settlements. We drove further out, away from the town and western influence, going northeast towards Korogwe until we once more saw Masai *morani* in their red cloaks and thatched huts, and in the distance ahead of us the cloud-shrouded Usambara Mountains. Here were wide plains and rolling countryside: ideal country for kudu, sable, buffalo and maybe even elephants, half a century and more ago. One could imagine these plains dotted with Thompson's gazelle and Grant's gazelle and impala. Somewhere in this area, northeast of Handeni, in late January 1934, Philip Percival established a new camp for the Hemingway party.

✳　✳　✳

Hemingway himself was still away from the bush, in Nairobi, convalescing from his attack of amoebic dysentery. While Charles Thompson, Ben Fourie and the rest of the safari party proceeded to a new camp on the Mosquito River in search of rhino, Pauline Hemingway and Percival drove along the exhausting road to Arusha to pay the convalescent a surprise visit. They were crushed to find that he was not there. But he soon returned, and the reunion was a happy one. The trio now rejoined Thompson and the others, relieved to be back pursuing their real goal in Africa.

The hunting was becoming problematic, however, as the competition between the two Americans hotted up. Hemingway was the better shot, fitter and tougher, but luck favoured Thompson. Time and again, Hemingway joyfully returned to camp with a fine trophy only to find that Thompson had bagged a specimen just that bit bigger and better. Hemingway's rhinoceros, for instance, had a seventeen-inch horn, but a couple of days later, Thompson topped it with a whopping twenty-three-incher. Ever the diplomat, Percival separated the two hunters during the day, but he could not prevent the evening postmortems when Hemingway would try, and fail, to come second with good grace. In *Green Hills*, he wrote self-deprecatingly about this, exaggerating his envy and bad temper for comic effect: "There we were, the three of us, wanting to congratulate, waiting to be good sports about this rhino whose smaller horn was longer than our big one, this huge, tear-eyed marvel of a rhino, this dead, head-severed dream rhino, and instead we spoke like people who were about to become seasick on a boat, or people who had suffered some heavy financial loss."[2]

Still, the rhino hunting was successful and Pauline was surprised to find

Charles Thompson, Ben Fourie, Philip Percival and Hemingway. Time and again, Hemingway joyfully returned to camp with a fine trophy only to find that Thompson had bagged a specimen just that bit bigger and better.

that the rhino was a clean animal, with a hide that was easy to cut through and white in colour. She was pleased that both men bagged one, even if Thompson had made her husband's rhino look so puny that he knew he "could never keep him in the same small town where we [both] lived."[3]

As for kudu, time was running out before heavy rains would make the roads impassable. The two kudu hunters had such little success in the nearby bush that Percival decided to shift the camp to Kijungu, a move that took a day and half, which they fervently hoped would improve their chances. At first, neither had any result, waiting long hours at a salt lick likely to attract kudu but returning empty handed to Pauline and Percival at the end of the day. Then, on February 11, Thompson came back in triumph with a pair of horns, long and twisted like exquisite wrought iron. Of course Hemingway's determination to get a fine kudu head now became all consuming. Only five full days of hunting remained, and the first drops of rain were beginning to fall. Hemingway's dogged, if enjoyable pursuit of kudu was acquiring an air of desperation.

The next day started well. Hemingway had spotted the "long, heart-shaped, fresh tracks" of four kudu bulls that had been at the salt lick during the night. He had a chance at a lesser kudu, but did not take the shot for fear of scaring off the greater kudu he hoped would return at dusk. But in the evening the elusive greater beast escaped again – this time frightened off by the sound of an engine. "Everything . . . that had been moving, in the bush on the flats, or coming down from the small hills through the trees, coming towards the salt, had halted at that exploding, clanking sound."[4] Hemingway's hopes had been dashed yet again.

☆   ☆   ☆

The day might have been wasted so far as kudu were concerned, but it paid dividends when Hemingway came to write *Green Hills of Africa*. The noisy truck belonged to a small man wearing a Tyrolean hat, *Lederhosen* and an open expression, named Hans Koritschoner. Remarkably, he recognized the name Hemingway from the German magazine *Der Querschnitt*, where the budding writer had published some bawdy poetry in the early 1920s before making his name. Koritschoner's cultural interests made him the perfect sparring partner (under the name Kandisky) for a Hemingway discourse on American literature; a version of their meeting opens the book. When Kandisky gets over his surprise that this Hemingway is indeed the famous writer he had once read in an obscure magazine, he finds it hard to believe that such an author could be genuinely interested in a lowbrow activity like kudu hunting. Hemingway responds that the sporting life and the life of the mind are complementary and equally valuable; that hunting in Tanganyika is as necessary to him as looking at great art in the Prado. This is not to denigrate writing, which is essential to his happiness: "I must write because if I do not write a certain amount I do not enjoy the rest of my life." It is simply a statement of fact. To Kandisky's question about what he really wants, he replies: "To write as well as I can and learn as I go along." But he won't let the German forget that hunting, the "silliness of kudu," as Kandisky calls it, is also vital. Writing must coexist with his life, he says, "which I enjoy and which is a damned good life."[5]

Green Hills of Africa was intended as a story of Hemingway's safari experience which would fuse life and art. Hemingway set out, as already noted in his brief foreword, "to write an absolutely true book to see whether the shape of a country and the pattern of a month's action can, if truly presented, compete with a work of the imagination." The narrative, carefully structured and tightly controlled, is centred on action. Hemingway uses the chasing of big game to sustain suspense, so that the reader feels sufficiently involved to keep turning the pages. But the reader must be willing, too, to follow the flashbacks to earlier parts of the safari that Hemingway throws in, and be ready to engage with the author's fairly lengthy digressions on literature and aesthetics. This "absolutely true book" is as elaborately evolved from its source material as the finest pair of kudu horns, as technically accomplished as anything in Hemingway's fiction. Of course, the immediacy – the sense of being there – that characterizes Hemingway's best work, is brilliantly in evidence.

As he tells Kandisky, writing and the rest of his "damned good life" are of equal but distinct importance to him. Hemingway had long been accustomed to enjoying both. In his working day, a morning of solid writing was generally followed by sport and relaxation all afternoon. Sometimes the proportions changed: the pull of action was stronger, or the writing was; but usually he maintained this balance, though never without difficulty. In 1935 he told the Russian critic Ivan Kashkeen that

> [a] life of action is easier to me than writing. I have a greater
> faculty for action than for writing. In action I do not worry

anymore. Once it is bad enough you get a sort of elation because there is nothing you can do except what you are doing and you have no responsibility. But writing is something that you can never do as well as it can be done. It is a perpetual challenge and it is more difficult than anything else that I have ever done – so I do it. And it makes me happy when I do it well.[6]

Yet it is not as if Hemingway saw no parallels between action and writing. At the end of a day's hunting, he writes in *Green Hills*, "feeling the cool wind of the night and smelling the good smell of Africa, I was altogether happy"[7] – but with this happiness came frustration at having performed less well than he should have. At the beginning of the book, Hemingway makes the comparison explicit:

Now it is pleasant to hunt something that you want very much over a long period of time, being outwitted, out-manoeuvered, and failing at the end of each day, but having the hunt and knowing every time you are out that, sooner or later, your luck will change and that you will get the chance that you are seeking. But it is not pleasant to have a time limit by which you must get your kudu or perhaps never get it, nor even see one. It is not the way hunting should be. It is too much like those boys who used to be sent to Paris with two years in which to make good as writers or painters after which, if they had not made good, they could go home and into their fathers' business. The way to hunt is for as long as you live against as long as there is such and such an animal; just as the way to paint is as long as there is you and colors and canvas, and to write as long as you can live and there is pencil and paper or ink or any machine to do it with, or anything you care to write about, and you feel a fool, and you are a fool, to do it any other way.[8]

Time and perseverance are needed for both art and sport. So too is the capacity to concentrate. Hunting is a matter of you, the animal, your gun and the time and effort involved in tracking and waiting. Writing is about you, a piece of paper and a pencil or some ink, patiently struggling with the ideas and feelings which "you care to write about." None of the distractions of everyday life, money, friendships, enmities and fame belongs in the relationship between the hunter and the quarry, the writer and his writing. Both hunter and writer share a solitary existence sustained by their willingness to keep hoping and trying for as long as it takes, in the knowledge that "your luck will change and that you will get the chance that you are seeking." One is reminded of Hemingway's contemporary in post-war Paris, James Joyce, who wrote in *A Portrait of the Artist as a Young Man*: "I will try to express myself in some mode of life or art as freely as I can and as wholly as I can, using for my defence the only arms I allow myself to use – silence, exile and cunning."[9]

The biographer Michael Reynolds, author of books covering the stages of Hemingway's life, argues (in *Hemingway: The 1930s*) that the connection between hunting and writing is even closer than his own statements suggest. In Reynolds's view,

> Trying to reach a prose beyond his earlier work, Hemingway uses the hunt, the quarry, and the hunter as metaphors for his trade. Hunter and writer are both professionals whose ground rules are stringent, whose conduct at parallel activities is meticulous, whose expectations for performance are high. The hunter pursues the lovely kudu, the promise of whose impossible spiraling horns makes the hunt valid. The writer is equally driven to write a book beyond anything he has done before, and in doing so exhausts an experience he can never again write. The greatest joy is in the pursuit of both kudu and book; the successful hunt puts one trophy on the wall, the other on the bookshelf. Leaving out most of the

safari's killing and using the kudu hunt as a guise, Hemingway
is writing a book about writing a book.[10]

Perhaps one may hazard that Hemingway aimed to hunt kudu with the
same determination and precision as he hunted for the right words in
his prose.

*   *   *

His run of bad luck in kudu hunting continued. The rains began to flood
the salt licks, and the available time for hunting was almost over. Percival,
anxious now about getting the safari party back to the coast, allowed
Hemingway one final sally. On February 16 he and the gun bearer
M'Cola took bedding and enough food for two days and set off in
search of kudu.

At last, on the penultimate day of the safari, Hemingway bagged two
beautiful kudu bulls. The wide, elaborate horns of the finer of the
two "rose in slow spirals that spreading made a turn, another turn, and
then curved delicately in to those smooth, ivory-like points."[11] Back
home in Key West, they would have pride of place on his wall. The
celebration that follows in *Green Hills*, as Hemingway unwinds around
the camp-fire with M'Cola and the trackers, is a safari idyll – an amalgam
of achievement, conviviality and the beauty of nature:

> In a little while they all began to come in carrying meat and
> the hides and then I was stretched out drinking beer and
> watching the fire and all around they were talking and
> roasting meat on sticks. It was getting cold and the night
> was clear and there was the smell of the roasting meat, the
> smell of the smoke of the fire, the smell of my boots steaming
> . . . But I could remember the odor of the kudu as he lay in
> the woods.[12]

The final day brings a sable cow and a victorious return to an enormously relieved Pauline and a delighted Percival. "'You'll never know what it meant to see that car come into the firelight with those damned horns sticking out,' Pop said. 'You old bastard.'" This time Hemingway is sure he has won the contest of trophies. Hearing that Thompson has bagged another kudu too, he decides he can afford to be magnanimous, since "I knew I had one no one could beat and I hoped he had a good one too." But once more he is mistaken. Thompson has gone one better. Hemingway sees "the biggest, widest, darkest, longest-curling, heaviest, most unbelievable pair of kudu horns in the world. Suddenly, poisoned with envy, I did not want to see mine again; never, never."[13]

He claims at the close of *Green Hills* to have recovered fully from his disappointment and swallowed his bitterness, and he certainly recovered sufficiently to look at the horns again and to take them home to Key West, where he would speak of the happy memories they conjured up. Martha Gellhorn, later the third Mrs Hemingway, told Pauline in a thank-you for her hospitality written in early 1937, that she felt she had become a "fixture" in the house at Key West, "like a kudu head."[14] However no amount of good sportsmanship could disguise the fact that Thompson's kudu horns spanned fifty-seven inches and Hemingway's only fifty-two. In the celebrated photograph of the men posing with their trophies on page 123, Percival and Thompson proudly brandish their kudu heads, and a smiling Hemingway holds not a kudu but an oryx head. Did he still fear the comparison?

* * *

On February 18, with the last trophies taken and the rains falling hard, the Hemingway party left for Kenya, passing through Tanga on the coast and Mombasa, on their way northwards to join Bror Blixen and Alfred Vanderbilt at the fishing resort of Malindi, there to drink, party and catch fish in memory of their eventful hunting safari. Our party too would follow the exact same route from Tanga onwards. But the first part of our route was different. The place-names fell on my ear with comforting familiarity, because I had come this way before, following Burton. We made good time to Tanga, where we stayed the night, before braving the hustle of Mombasa and arriving at the cooler oceanside villages of Kilifi and Malindi.

In the colonial period, these two places, bywords for their fishing and beautiful setting, were the haunts of the hedonistic "Happy Valley set", led by Joss Erroll until his murder in 1941. The woman at the centre of this notorious scandal, still unsolved and discussed even today in Kenya as mentioned earlier, was Diana Broughton, who had a passionate affair with Erroll. (The last word on the case used to be James Fox's *White Mischief*, until the recent publication of Errol Trebezinski's *The Life and Death of Lord Erroll*.) It was her adopted daughter, Snoo Colville, who by chance told me her late mother had been very keen on fishing and that the last of her boats, the *White Bear*, was now owned by a hotel in the resort of Watamu called Hemingway's.

Inevitably, I had to visit this place. But it turned out, as we chatted to the manager of Hemingway's, Gary Cullen, that the man himself never actually fished out of Watamu – he only drank at the hotel, which was formerly known as the Seafarers. And despite the fact that the hotel is named in Hemingway's honour, Cullen had little time for the American writer. He didn't mince words when he told us, "Basically Hemingway was extremely unpopular in this country. He was such a pig! Drinking, carousing, self-centred . . . He just pissed people off. If anyone was more successful than him, he became unbearable. Everyone wanted to treat him as a hero, but however hard they tried they eventually couldn't stand him."

In Malindi, where Hemingway, Percival, Blixen and Vanderbilt fished by day and caroused by night, one of his drinking spots was Lawford's Hotel, though he never mentions it by name in his writings. The place is a run-down relic now, rather shabby and even squalid, nothing like the way it must have been in its glory days. But the bar is still there, and I could visualize Hemingway at its sweeping, semi-circular counter, with a drink in one hand and the other hand stretched out wide to demonstrate the size of the fish he had caught that day.

In Malindi Hemingway and friends fished by day and caroused by night.

Here at last was a sporting activity he knew better than Percival. Hemingway introduced the white hunter to deep-sea fishing, and Percival went on to develop a life-long passion for it. About big-game hunting Hemingway once joked in a letter to *Esquire* that the notes he planned to write about elephant hunting would be like the "campaign impressions of a bloke who has never seen a major engagement."[15] In the same mood, and in the same letter, he talked of his hero Percival's efforts with rod and line:

One night when we were eating supper at Mombasa after fishing, A. V. [Vanderbilt] and Mr. P. [Percival] and I were talking about writing these letters and I suggested Alfred write one about hunting elephant with Blix before he started to write on racing. I was writing on rhino and buffalo, etc., I said. Mr. P., who was on his first deep-sea fishing trip, didn't say much, but the next day we got into a big school of large dolphin and caught about fifteen before the lousy

Here at last was a sporting activity Hemingway knew better than Percival. On the Kenyan coast, after the end of the safari, he introduced his white hunter to deep-sea fishing, and Percival went on to develop a lifelong passion for it.

boat broke down. Mr. P. got so excited that his legs shook, he screwed the reel brake backwards until it stuck, he had dolphin humping into, out of, and over the boat. Sometimes he jerked the bait out of their mouths; occasionally he let them swallow it, but always he had a dolphin jumping on his line.

"How do you like it, Pop?" I asked him.

"God," he said, "I haven't had so much fun since the day you shot the buffalo." Then, a little later, "I'm going to write an article on it for *Esquire*. Call it Dolphin Fishing by One Who Knows."

At the end of the fishing junket, the Hemingways packed up their trophies and their diaries and sailed back to Europe. At the end of *our* stay in Malindi, we packed the Land Rovers with our equipment and my travel acquisitions – dolls, spears, charms, Mbulu axes. Joerg, who had come down with a bad chest infection, was coughing constantly, but there was no time to waste. We were expected once more at Lake Naivasha. There I was hoping to take stock of what I had so far learned about Hemingway in Africa, and prepare for the last leg of our journey around Tsavo.

CHAPTER 6

Experience Distilled

Forget your personal tragedy. We are all bitched from the start and you especially have to be hurt like hell before you can write seriously. But when you get the damned hurt use it – don't cheat with it. Be as faithful to it as a scientist – but don't think anything is of any importance because it happens to you or anyone belonging to you.

ERNEST HEMINGWAY TO F. SCOTT FITZGERALD

May 28 1934[1]

Since I had always intended to cover both Hemingway safaris in one trip, vaulting a gap of twenty years (from 1934 to 1953), I was now in the middle of my journey while contemplating the closure of Hemingway's first one. How did he, when he returned to the United States, set about moulding his teeming memories of Africa into *Green Hills of Africa* and a little later (in 1936) a classic short story, "The Snows of Kilimanjaro"? (And of course "The Short Happy Life of Francis Macomber.") To attempt an answer to this question is a challenge, not only because major writers are generally secretive about their creative processes, but also because it brings one up against the deepest anxieties of Hemingway's life, anxieties which I think nagged at his mind and body like a hyena gnawing at its own guts until, ultimately, he silenced them with a gun to his head.

Hemingway began to draft Green Hills of Africa *– working title "The Highland of Africa" – as soon as he was back in Key West. Scribner published it in the autumn of 1935.*

Hemingway began to draft *Green Hills of Africa* – working title, "The Highland of Africa" – as soon as he was back in Key West. Apart from "pencil and paper," he possessed that other major requirement of the writer that he would mention near the beginning of *Green Hills*: something "you care to write about."[2] He also had a stack of books on big-game hunting at his side, plus photographs and notes taken on safari (but no journal). Despite a summer full of visitors and distractions, by the end of the autumn the African book was nearly ready, and he was sure it would meet with the critics' approval; he considered it to be the best book he had written. When Scribner published in the autumn of 1935, Hemingway went to New York to celebrate what he expected would be glowing reviews.

His hopes were not entirely fulfilled. The critics admired the book's evocation of landscape and its sharp observation of wildlife, but they resented the pontification, the lordly disdain for other writers (especially those living in New York!). Perhaps the long, opinionated dialogue about life and art with Kandisky in the opening of the book had set Hemingway up for a fall. He certainly does not pull his punches in writing about the condition of American literature, even about such revered figures as Emerson, Hawthorne and Whittier. According to Hemingway, their works lacked the stylistic qualities closest to his heart: the frankness of the vernacular and a sure evocation of the physical world. These authors "did not use the words that people always have used in speech, the words that survive in language. Nor would you gather that they had bodies. They had minds, yes. Nice, dry, clean minds."[3] The only American authors who garnered his ungrudging respect were Mark Twain (Hemingway insisted that all American literature came from *Huckleberry Finn*), Stephen Crane, who shared Hemingway's interest in bravery, masculinity and war, and Henry James, who would be an important influence on "The Snows of Kilimanjaro." Literary critics, too, were condemned as destructive influences on writers. As Hemingway explains to Kandisky, most American authors are destroyed, "by the first money, the first praise, the first attack, the first time they find they cannot write, or the first time they cannot do anything else."[4]

Hemingway was in the habit of biting the hands that had fed him, so it was perhaps ingenuous to have expected the critics to adore his latest effort. The reviews were by no means bad, but they made clear that readers did not want another work of non-fiction from Hemingway – the book before *Green Hills*, *Death in the Afternoon*, had analysed bullfighting – but rather another novel. Seldom satisfied with anything less than unalloyed praise, he sank into a depression.

His frame of mind during the writing and publication of *Green Hills* follows a pattern of mood swings that has been spotted by his recent biographers, notably Michael Reynolds. Energy and happiness during the writing of a book were often followed by depression soon after publication. In 1935–36, his black mood was so bad he began to mutter to friends about suicide. However, the depression did not lead to lethargy, staunching the flow of his writing: it was in this period that he wrote "The Short Happy Life of Francis Macomber" and "The Snows of Kilimanjaro."

Where "Macomber" is a highly dramatic tale of adventure, danger and sudden, bloody death, "Kilimanjaro" offers practically no action, only the internal workings of a man's mind as he waits for rescue or death in gangrene-enforced immobility. Harry, the central character, is a writer who has wasted his talent – like the American authors mentioned in *Green Hills* who were destroyed by various enemies of promise. In Harry's case, the soft life has seduced him away from writing. Married to a rich wife, he is at liberty to do anything he likes. But instead of becoming a writer, he becomes a fritterer. At first he lays the blame for his lack of literary output on his wife, Helen. Even though she shares his enthusiasms and always puts his needs first, Harry insists that her money has ruined him and tells himself that the only reasons he sticks with her are that "she was richer, because she was very pleasant and appreciative and because she never made scenes."[5] The jibes he throws at her as she tries to comfort him, and her emollient replies, are the sole dialogue in the story. The rest comprises Harry's inner soliloquies and some long flashbacks to his earlier life, to experiences he knows he should have written about and now never will.

These memories mirror many of Hemingway's own preoccupations. Harry remembers a Turkish attack in the First World War and its aftermath: "he had seen the things that he could never think of and later still he had seen much worse."[6] He remembers the exhilaration of skiing on Alpine snow "as smooth to see as cake frosting and as light as powder" and "the noiseless rush the speed made as you dropped down like a bird."[7] And he recalls, after quarrelling with a woman in Paris, whoring in Constantinople with a "hot Armenian slut." He remembers stories he has overheard, and details of appearances, behaviours and locations – all the material his writer's eye has noted for future use, now redundant.

Harry attaches special significance to his memories of Paris. He claims, despite the evidence we already have of his excellent memory, not to recall the Paris he shared with his second wife Helen. This was a city of elegant hotels, lavish restaurants and nothing that touched his heart – the way of life he blames for the destruction of his talent. But the Parisian streets where he lived in comparative poverty with his first wife are still fresh in his mind. "There never was another part of Paris that he loved like that, the sprawling trees, the old white plastered houses painted brown below, the long green of the autobus in that round square, the purple flower dye upon the paving . . ." In the simplicity of his youth in Paris, Harry implies that life was more productive, that he felt more keenly. "And in that poverty, and in that quarter across the street from a Boucherie Chevaline and a wine co-operative he had written the start of all he was to do."[8] This Paris, and his tiny apartment there, Harry invests with a lost happiness and an intense nostalgia.

The quarter of Paris Hemingway describes is the one in which he actually lived with Hadley Richardson, his first wife, and enjoyed his first literary success. "The Snows of Kilimanjaro" is Hemingway's first writing to try to recapture the Paris of his twenties and explain its special atmosphere and significance. As he grew older, he made the attempt with increasing frequency, culminating in his gossipy memoir *A Moveable Feast*, published in 1964 after his death.

It is tricky to discern where autobiography ends and fiction begins in "The Snows of Kilimanjaro." According to Hemingway himself, it was a rich woman in New York who invited him to tea in April 1934 and offered to sponsor another safari, who started the process of imagination that led to his writing the story. Though he spurned her offer, he found himself day-dreaming about what might have happened to him had he agreed.

Like his character Harry, Hemingway saw fighting and destruction in the world war that he could never forget; he knew too all about the feel of different kinds of snow under his skis; and we know he began his career in Paris with his first wife. There are certainly some similarities, as well, between Helen of the story and Pauline, Hemingway's second wife, who had once worked for the Paris edition of *Vogue*. Pauline was rich – her father had made a fortune on the St. Louis grain exchange; she was comfortable among the rich and celebrated as Hadley Richardson had never been; and her money made it possible for Hemingway to live far more expensively than hitherto. But there are major differences between Helen and Pauline. For one thing, Helen is described as being a very good shot, which Pauline was not; for another, the marriage to Pauline is generally a tender and happy one as described in *Green Hills*, unlike the marriage in "Kilimanjaro."

Helen, one feels, is primarily a fictional device to show up Harry's failings. He makes of her a scapegoat, though the reader can see she is not to blame – and so, in the bitter end, can Harry himself. While it is true that her money has bought the luxury that has put fat on Harry's soul, depriving him of the isolation and asceticism that Hemingway thought necessary to the serious writer – "each day of not writing, of comfort, of being that which he despised, dulled his ability and softened his will to work so that, finally, he did no work at all"[9] – it is nobody's fault but his own that Harry has succumbed. Having berated his wife for being a "rich bitch"[10] and the "destroyer of his talent,"[11] he pulls himself up and admits, if only to himself, the injustice of these taunts: "Nonsense. He had destroyed his talent himself. Why should he blame this woman because she kept him well?"[12] His criticizing of her reveals much more about him than about her. If we read "The Snows of Kilimanjaro" autobiographically, the story tells us about Hemingway's fear of death, wasted talent and lost opportunities, not about his wife Pauline.

The women characters in both "Kilimanjaro" and "Macomber" are key figures, but it is true that they are important for the way their men react to them, rather than for themselves. In neither story do we get inside the women's heads. For Hemingway's subject here is manhood and a man's being true to his own nature and talent. Without the trappings of civilization and never far from the possibility of death, his male characters must face themselves, without female support and comfort. And so the female characters are given only enough depth to make them dramatically effective in highlighting the strengths and weaknesses of the male characters. Whether this attitude makes the writer of these stories a misogynist, as is often suggested, seems to me debatable. But what is beyond doubt is that on his real-life safaris – the second one as much as the first – Hemingway made a constant effort to ensure the pleasure of his wives; which is more the behaviour of a gentleman than of a macho man. His wives are an essential part of his non-fiction about Africa, and it is remarkable that he knew, instinctively, that this should be so.

The main *literary* influence on "The Snows of Kilimanjaro" comes, I believe, from two male writers: Henry James and F. Scott Fitzgerald. Of the three American writers the author extols to Kandisky in *Green Hills*, James seems the most different from Hemingway. What could be further from Hemingway's spare stories than James's minute examinations of class-ridden society, his privileging of the interior life over the world of action, and his intricate, allusive, spreading, often orotund sentences? But as the Hemingway biographer Carlos Baker has pointed out, both James and Hemingway were fascinated with the American in Europe and the position of the artist in society. Moreover, "The Snows of Kilimanjaro" shows obvious similarities to "The Lesson of the Master," James's ambiguous tale about the sacrifices required for literary excellence; as well as the more tangential influence of James's ghost story "The Jolly Corner."

The "Master" of the first story's title is Henry St. George, a famous author. For all his acclaim, though, St. George insists to his young disciple Paul Overt that he is no master, really nothing more than a "successful charlatan."[13] At the start of his career he did produce a few first-class books, but his recent work has fallen off considerably, a circumstance he blames on marriage, family and the demands of material prosperity. St. George tells the young writer, "It's so much easier to be worse – heaven knows I've found it so . . . But you *must* be better, you really must keep it up. I haven't of course. It's very difficult – that's the devil of the whole thing, keeping it up."[17] Hemingway has the same idea in *Green Hills* when he tells Kandisky that the true writer must have "an absolute conscience as unchanging as the standard meter in Paris, to prevent faking" and that only such a commitment to his work will allow him to survive the pitfalls surrounding writing. The overwhelming necessity for the true writer is to "get his work done."[15] Since St. George believes in Overt's talent, he warns him, "Don't become in your old age what I have in mine – the depressing, the deplorable illustration of the worship of false gods!"[16] Which is precisely what Harry in "Kilimanjaro" recognizes that he has become, to the detriment of his writing.

This advice is given after St. George learns that Overt is in love. It is largely a warning against marriage, which the older man believes saps the writer's all-important independence: "Let him have all the passions he likes – if he only keeps his independence. He must be able to be poor."[17] But then, at the end of the story, James introduces a twist. St. George marries the girl Overt loves, in an act that can be read either as entirely selfish or as entirely unselfish. There is no ambiguity, however, in the older man's belief that in achieving wealth and a happy family, he has gained everything but the "great thing." This is, for an artist, the "sense of having done the best – the sense which is the real life of the artist and the absence of which is his death, of having drawn from his intellectual instrument the finest music that nature had hidden in it, of having played it as it should be played. He either does that or he doesn't – and if he doesn't he isn't worth speaking of."[18] The "great thing" is what Harry in "Kilimanjaro" has sacrificed, and what Hemingway too believed in.

In "The Jolly Corner," James writes of Spencer Brydon, an American who returns to New York after many years. He begins to take an interest in the Jolly Corner, a house he lived in as a young man and still owns, and soon the house becomes an obsession, because its presence forces him to consider how his life might have turned out had he stayed in New York. Once he opens himself up to speculation, Brydon "found himself considering a circumstance that, after his first and comparatively vague apprehension of it, produced in him the start that often attends some

Both Henry James and Hemingway were fascinated with the American in Europe and the position of the artist in society. James's stories influenced "The Snows of Kilimanjaro."

pang of recollection, the violent shock of having ceased happily to forget."[19] He comes to believe that "I had then a strange *alter ego* deep down somewhere within me, as the full-blown flower is in the small tight bud, and that I just took the course, I just transferred him to the climate, that blighted him for once and for ever."[20] He suspects that the *alter ego* is haunting the house in the form of a ghost, and so he takes to visiting the Jolly Corner at night, to catch a glimpse of the apparition. He fears the ghost, yet wants to meet it, driven by a question: "What would it have made of me, what would it have made of me? I keep for ever wondering, all idiotically; as if I could possibly know!"[21] Eventually he hunts it down and confronts it in the story's climactic scene. Afterwards, Brydon seems almost reborn, and he achieves happiness with the woman he loves. It appears that the ghost embodied a half-born younger self which Brydon had to exorcise in order to live completely in the present. As the author noted in a preface, "the important thing about 'The Jolly Corner' is that the hero turns the tables on the apparition which ought, by rights, to appall him. He achieves a victory over it by the fact that it is more affected by their encounter than he is."

The proximity of death forces Hemingway's Harry to face his own *alter ego*. He deliberately calls up his youth, and the memory of this former, aborted self – the poor writer, full of promise, observant and keen witted, ambitious to excel – provokes an urgent soul-destroying guilt in Harry. His flashbacks are a reminder of a life only partially lived, because he gave up trying to fulfil his destiny to write. The conclusion of James's story certainly differs from that of Hemingway, as does the tone – for the confrontation with the former self does not bring new life to Harry, as it does to Brydon – but the basic idea that a suppressed self can return in later life to disturb the complacent existing self, is common to both stories.

As for Scott Fitzgerald's influence on "The Snows of Kilimanjaro," it was very different to that of James, being directly related to Fitzgerald's personality and friendship with Hemingway. The two of them met in Paris in the 1920s, and Fitzgerald, who was on the point of publishing

The Great Gatsby, helped to launch Hemingway by introducing him to his editor, Maxwell Perkins at Scribner. But as Hemingway's literary star rose, Fitzgerald's, in Hemingway's view, fell, and after the publication of *Tender is the Night* in 1934, he came to regard Fitzgerald as a fine example of a talented writer's destruction by the imperatives of wealth and fame.

In *Green Hills*, Hemingway explains to Kandisky that a writer of a good book will make money, increase his standard of living, and get caught. "They have to write to keep up their establishments, their wives, and so on, and they write slop. It is slop not on purpose but because it is hurried." Reading the critics is deadly, too, because if writers "believe the critics when they say they are great then they must believe them when they say they are rotten and they lose confidence. At present we have two good writers who cannot write because they have lost confidence through reading critics."[22] He meant (but did not name) Fitzgerald and Sherwood Anderson. To Hemingway, Fitzgerald had squandered his talent by writing trashy magazine stories to make some quick money so that he and his wife Zelda could afford to live in fabulous decadence.

Scott Fitzgerald's influence on "The Snows of Kilimanjaro" was very different to that of Henry James, being directly related to Fitzgerald's personality and friendship with Hemingway.

An obvious jibe at Fitzgerald occurs in "The Snows of Kilimanjaro." Harry is made to criticize a friend, "poor Julian," who was so in awe of the very rich that when he found out that they were not in fact "different" after all but simply had more money than other people, the realization destroyed him. Hemingway felt justified in stinging an old friend as a result of reading Fitzgerald's notorious "Crack-Up" essays, which were published in *Esquire* in 1936 at the very time Hemingway was writing his African stories. Here Fitzgerald took a scalpel to himself, dissecting his own mental breakdown, personal flaws and artistic failures. Such explicit, unforgiving confessions were unprecedented in American literature – though they have since spawned an entire genre of writing. To Hemingway, however, they were little more than public whining, and his reaction was one of furious dislike.

In reacting so strongly, he may have feared his own crack-up. Reading the essays probably forced Hemingway to consider more deeply a serious writer's obligation to his talent. Jeffrey Meyers, in his biography of Fitzgerald, goes so far as to argue that "The Snows of Kilimanjaro" is not just an examination of the guilt that a wealthy writer like Fitzgerald might have felt about betraying himself, it also bears a marked literary resemblance to Fitzgerald's confessional essays:

> This story, though written at the height of Hemingway's worldly success, reveals his anxiety about his incipient moral corruption (symbolized by the hero's gangrene) and predicts his failure as a writer and his spiritual death. One of Hemingway's greatest works, it is in fact a more subtle, covert and artistically sophisticated version of "The Crack-Up": an incisive confrontation of failure and analysis of what had caused it.[23]

CHAPTER 7

Out of Africa

*I had been a fool not to have stayed on in Africa and instead
had gone back to America where I had killed my home-
sickness for Africa in different ways. Then before I could get
back came the Spanish war and I became involved in what
was happening to the world and I had stayed with that
for better and for worse until I had finally come back.
It had not been easy to get back nor to break the chains
of responsibility that are built up, seemingly, as lightly as
spider webs but that hold like steel cables.*

ERNEST HEMINGWAY
True at First Light[1]

Hemingway left Kenya in 1934 with the firm intention of returning.
Africa held out the possibility of a simpler, leaner, more intense existence,
far removed from the superficialities and superfluities of life as a celebrity
American writer. It had everything he needed for a fulfilling life, he
asserted in *Green Hills of Africa*: "Here there was game, plenty of birds,
and I liked the natives. Here I could shoot and fish. That, and writing,
and reading, and seeing pictures was all I cared about doing. And I
could remember all the pictures."[2]

While still on safari, already he was looking ahead to a second safari.
As he told *Esquire* readers in one of his letters, "We plan to go out again
to Kenya for six months next year to try to get a really good [elephant],

*Ancestral tribal lands in Africa are disappearing under constant pressure from
all sides – agricultural corporations, tourists, professional hunters and
government resettlement programmes.*

to hunt buffalo and rhino, and to see how far wrong first impressions of these were, and to try to get a good bull sable."[3]

But as things turned out, neither the short-term plan for a safari nor the long-term desire to live in Africa came to fruition. Hemingway did not return there in 1935, nor indeed for nearly twenty years; instead he got caught up in private and public events both in America and Europe. And although he did find a dwelling place away from Key West that combined natural beauty with the potential for some of the things he "cared about doing,"[4] (*Green Hills* again) – that location was in Cuba, not Africa. He never made Africa his home.

Martha Gellhorn, who was briefly mentioned earlier in relation to the kudu hunt, came into his life at this time. The two of them met at Sloppy

Martha Gelhorn, the woman who would become Hemingway's third wife, was ten years his junior, fiercely independent and a published author when they met in 1936.

Joe's bar – Hemingway's regular Key West watering hole – in late 1936. Like his first and second wives, Hadley and Pauline, Martha came from St. Louis. Unlike them, however, the woman who would become Hemingway's third wife was ten years his junior, fiercely independent and a published author. Gellhorn's second book, *The Trouble I've Seen*, a collection of short stories, had been highly praised – enough for Hemingway to recognize her name – but she knew she still had much to learn. Their initial relationship was therefore that of a literary master and an eager admirer (her first book, a novel, had an epigraph by Hemingway) who looked to Hemingway for encouragement and inspiration.

Gellhorn had always wanted to be a foreign correspondent; her life plan, as cited in Bernice Kert's *The Hemingway Women*, was "to go everywhere, see everything, and write about it."[5] And she pretty well managed this too, covering the Spanish Civil War, the Second World War, the Six-Day War of 1967 and the Vietnam War, as well as filing reports in peacetime from all over the world and writing several novels to boot. From the first it was clear that she would never be a submissive helpmeet to a husband, happy to live only for him. Maria, the heroine of Hemingway's novel *For Whom the Bell Tolls*, may share Gellhorn's physical attributes, notably her never-ending legs and glorious hair, but she lacks her self-assurance and self-reliance. Intelligent, sharp and beautiful, Gellhorn was one of the few people in the world completely unimpressed by Hemingway's fame. And having led a life as varied and colourful as his, she later came to resent the shadow that her marriage to him cast over her career. Only now, with the publication of Carl Rollyson's biography of Gellhorn, *Beautiful Exile*, has she begun to gain the recognition she deserves.

The affair between her and Hemingway blossomed in the Spanish Civil War. Gellhorn was in Spain covering the war for *Collier's*, Hemingway for the North American Newspaper Alliance. He greatly admired her courage. Away from home and Pauline, free of all responsibilities, amid the falling shells and fighting, with the prospect of imminent death charging the present with excitement, Hemingway and Gellhorn fell in love. Pauline could only watch as the same situation that had developed between Hadley, Ernest and herself in Paris a decade earlier developed again, this time with her in the role of wife. Her fight for her marriage eventually proved futile. Fourteen years after she first met Hemingway, the couple separated, and in 1940, Gellhorn and Hemingway married and set up home in Cuba.

But their relations were troubled from the start. Hemingway needed a wife who would put his needs first. He grew jealous of a career that took her away from him for long intervals, and he resented his needing her more than she seemed to need him. Gellhorn, in turn, deplored his temper, slovenliness, heavy drinking, exaggerated anecdotes and increasing indulgence of a coterie of admirers who obsequiously reflected his greatness back at him.

Their disagreements came to a head during the Second World War. Gellhorn rushed to Europe to cover the fighting and exhorted her husband to go too. Uncomfortable with the idea of his living in the lap of luxury in Cuba while his beloved Europe fell apart, she told him it was his duty to go – the war needed his talent. His reluctance provoked her further disapproval, and although Hemingway did eventually fly over, and reported on the Normandy landings and the liberation of Paris in 1944, his third marriage was at an end. When Gellhorn heard that he had been seeing another woman in London, Mary Welsh, she was delighted, for now he would have to give her a divorce. Martha Gellhorn seems to have been the only female intimate of Hemingway to have parted from him without regret.

Clearly she was not among those who subscribed to the Hemingway myth, which by the mid-1940s was fully formed. Ever since he was a young writer in the 1920s, Hemingway had wanted to be famous, and he always worked hard to cultivate his own reputation. His non-fiction of the 1930s – *Death in the Afternoon*, *Green Hills of Africa*, the letters

Ever since he was a young writer in the 1920s, Hemingway had wanted to be famous, and he always worked hard to cultivate his legendary reputation.

for *Esquire* and the reports from the Spanish Civil War – all presented a particular persona to the public which Hemingway was happy to conspire with. Here was a man who relished manliness and courage, adventure and sportsmanship, whisky and women, but who also displayed an artistic sensibility, a strong work ethic and a belief in the value of the written word. "The legend of Hemingway is modern-Byronic. It is made up of tales of drinking, bull-fighting, carnal experiences in the war, rough talk and bad manners, and then wine and more wine," the critic Lawrence Conrad wrote in 1934. And this list omitted the latest Hemingway obsession: big-game hunting in Africa. Yet Conrad's "modern-Byronic" label makes a less obvious point: that Hemingway was not just an adventurous romantic idol but at the same time an ambitious, dedicated writer.

In the 1940s, the legend warped into something closer to mock-Byronic. The writer was often neglected as the newspapers and magazines concentrated on Hemingway, the tough-talking action hero. Inevitably, a much-travelling, hard-drinking, often-married, macho man made for much racier copy than a gifted writer working at home in his study. Hemingway's complex personality was frequently reduced by journalists to a handful of immediately recognizable characteristics; his personal renown (often his notoriety) overrode his literary achievements. When he was awarded the Nobel prize in 1954, *Time* magazine reported the event not under "Books" but under "Heroes." Photographs of Hemingway, too, tended to focus on the sportsman, not the writer. Although there are one or two famous shots of the writer bent over his desk, grappling with dialogue or struggling for the perfect phrase, "Hemingway" as a name recalls images of the weather-beaten fisherman proudly dwarfed by a massive marlin, or the rugged, khaki-clad hunter striding, gun in hand, through the African bush – more than it does the writer.

Notwithstanding the Nobel, the years between his first and second safaris saw his celebrity rise but his literary output decline, as did the critical reception for his writing. *The Essential Hemingway*, still available

When Hemingway was awarded the Nobel prize in 1954, Time *magazine reported the event not under "Books" but under "Heroes."*

in paperback, contains no work written after *For Whom the Bell Tolls*, his spectacularly successful novel of the Spanish Civil War, published in 1940. Ten years passed before his next novel, *Across the River and Into the Trees*, a poorly received romance between an ageing colonel and a beautiful Venetian girl. In the meantime, he published little except his journalistic pieces about the Second World War, ego-stained reports from Europe angled at the folks back home, which naturally added to his reputation as a man of action. As Malcolm Bradbury, critic and novelist, remarked during Hemingway's birth centenary in 1999,

In his later years Hemingway became an aggressive, boastful

figure, patriarchally celebrating his skills and strengths, and establishing competitive dominance and control over those who surrounded him. He began to strut the world's landscapes as if no one understood them but he. He was Papa Hemingway, instructing, commanding, ruling, everywhere acquiring respectful acolytes, deferential *amigos*, multiple 'daughters', surrogate 'wives'.[6]

This picture of him strutting "the world's landscapes," including of course East Africa in 1953–54, is one that intrigues me. Certainly he was no explorer, not a man like Livingstone or Burton always looking for new discoveries, usually in uncharted territory, and motivated by a certain necessary humility. Yet he was more than a mere adventurer. As a *writer* about Africa, I think Hemingway deserves to be called an explorer, even if he was only an adventurer in his travels and personal life on safari.

The relevant issue here seems to be whether or not Hemingway's writings left their mark on the country he had grown to love, in exchange for the indelible impression Africa had made on him. As Karen Blixen puts it in *Out of Africa*, "I know a song of Africa – I thought – of the giraffe, of the African new moon lying on her back . . . Does Africa know a song of me?"[7] With Hemingway, too, Africa did know and still does know.

More than any other writer, including Blixen, Hemingway established Africa in the American consciousness. He made it into a land of mystery and adventure. Rather as, towards the end of the nineteenth century, Henry Rider Haggard's adventure romance *King Solomon's Mines,* fired the British imagination and encouraged scores of young Englishmen to try their luck in Africa, so Hemingway's African writings and the films based on his safari stories made African tourism fashionable in America. If you type 'safari' into an internet search engine, you will find half-a-dozen tour operators advertising "Hemingway safaris" that promise the adventurous that they will follow in the great man's footsteps, tread his green hills and unwind in the shadow of Kilimanjaro. "It was because of Hemingway that America developed its huge interest in Africa," said Alwyn Smith, the father-in-law of my safari guide Joerg, when we talked at his house on Lake Naivasha. "The safari outfitters Kerr and Downey saw an upsurge in business following the publication of Hemingway's safari book and short stories. Hemingway started a trend that Hollywood latched on to, making films like *Mogambo*. Theodore Roosevelt and the Prince of Wales might have made Africa attractive to the rich elite, but it was Hemingway who really popularized it as a desirable tourist destination."

Many of Hemingway's writings were made into movies, such was the wild success in America of his novels and short stories. There are more than a dozen star-studded films based on Hemingway novels and short stories such as *A Farewell to Arms*, *For Whom the Bell Tolls*, "The Killers," *The Sun Also Rises* and *To Have and Have Not*, of which two, *The Macomber Affair* and *The Snows of Kilimanjaro*, are set in Africa.

In truth, most of these movies are travesties of the original work. The only fine film made from a Hemingway book is Howard Hawks's *To Have and Have Not* (1944); and the original novel is barely recognizable. The popularity of Hemingway's books with Hollywood producers is easily understandable – they are full of heroism, romance and tragedy – but it is clear that the books do not transfer easily to the silver screen. Hemingway's own "iceberg theory" proposes that only ten per cent of a good story is directly visible in the prose. Few film-makers understood that the real appeal of his stories does not spring from any exciting action scenes directly described in words, but from the implied – and often unpredictable – human psychology that drives the action.

Thus, the advertising poster for Zoltan Korda's *The Macomber Affair* (1946) reduces its protagonists to "A Man" (Wilson), "A Vixen" (Margot) and "A Coward" (Macomber), leaving little doubt as to the hero. In Korda's movie, there is no ambiguity surrounding Macomber's death as there is in "The Short Happy Life of Francis Macomber." The killing of Macomber by his wife is presented as a pure accident – the

The advertising poster for Zoltan Korda's The Macomber Affair *(1946) reduces its protagonists to "A Man" (Wilson), "A Vixen" (Margot) and "A Coward" (Macomber), leaving little doubt as to the hero.*

result of his foolhardiness in confronting the wounded buffalo – which conveniently leaves Margot to fall innocently into the muscular arms of the white hunter (played by a dashing Gregory Peck), the man she really loves.

The film version of "The Snows of Kilimanjaro," made in 1952, takes even more liberties with its source – with the overriding aim of ensuring a happy ending rather than of presenting human psychology as it actually is. The suffering writer Harry (again played by Peck) comes to terms with his colourful past and romances in Europe – which naturally introduces

The film version of "The Snows of Kilimanjaro," made in 1952, takes even more liberties with its source – with the overriding aim of ensuring a happy ending rather than of presenting human psychology as it actually is.

the charms of Ava Gardner, Susan Hayward and Hildegard Neff (Knef) – and determines to work at his writing rather than succumb to *la dolce vita*. Having reached this level of self-awareness and devotion to his work, he is able to recover from his gangrene and make up with his rich wife. As the credits roll the hero lives on, his literary potential destined not to be wasted after all. Or as one unimpressed film critic put it: "Peck's weighty Harry Street remains resolutely aloof, to the point where he will not deign to expire."[8] Hemingway himself was irritated by an ending that sacrificed the truth so that the cinema audience could leave with a feel-good glow. Hollywood had falsified his story just as it had faked Africa itself by shooting much of the movie with studio backdrops consisting of an unconvincing mixture of a giant painting of Kilimanjaro and back-projections of wildlife footage.

As for Karen Blixen's *Out of Africa*, when Hollywood got around to adapting it in the mid-1980s, times had changed – Kenya was no longer a British colony and big-game hunting was out of fashion, as were studio shoots – so the film-makers decided to shoot on location and concentrate on the natural beauty and romance of East Africa. When the movie was first shown in Nairobi, the ticket line stretched for blocks and audiences rose to their feet at the end to applaud the film. The acting (especially in the two male roles of Bror Blixen and Denys Finch Hatton) was not very realistic, but for anyone who longs to relive African sights, sounds and smells, this is the film to watch and watch again; the next-best thing to being in the bush. For me, it brings back those early mornings on safari with the rising sun, the chorus of mourning doves and the fragrance of wood smoke in my nostrils. And the smell of dust: dry and hot as you charge out onto the open plains; clinging to all orifices in the towns and villages, filthy with spit, urine and garbage; and moist, heavy and soothing with the approach of rain – which I love. I suppose the last of these smells is really the smell of the wind that brings the rain, the smell of rain falling far away, soaking the distant red earth. I often lift my face to the downpour when it comes and let it rinse off the dust and grime of a journey. Within minutes of its stopping, one's skin and clothes are completely dry. It is experiences like these that cause outsiders who love Africa to be obsessed with the idea of return, even before – as with Hemingway in 1934 – they have actually left African shores.

Interestingly, since she never visited Africa with Hemingway, his divorced wife Martha Gellhorn felt the pull too. She made her first trip only in 1962, intending to cross the continent from west to east, hoping to escape civilization and find the 'real' Africa; Hemingway's comparatively comfortable safari lifestyle was to have no place in her expedition. West

Africa did not appeal to her, but like him and countless others, she fell in love with the gentler climate and breathtaking landscapes of the east. Her writing about Kenya is eloquent in her autobiography, though tinged with a sadness that she could never quite penetrate the country's secrets:

> The love affair with Africa was long, obsessed and unrequited, lasting off and on for thirteen years. Africa remained out of reach except for moments of union, when walking on the long empty beach at sunrise or sunset, when watching the night sky. Or later, when I had built my two-room tenth permanent residence high in the Rift Valley and could look at four horizons, drunk on space and drunk on silence. Or always, driving alone on the backroads, when Africa offered me as a gift its surprises, the beautiful straying animals, the shape of the mountains, wild flowers.[9]

This house, where Gellhorn settled for some years and wrote *The Weather in Africa*, was built for her on top of Mount Longonot. The secluded location was ludicrously high – she was advised against it but insisted – and although she had friends and was a popular guest, it was not a very sociable existence. Beryl Markham lived close by, but she and Gellhorn met only once. (In an introduction to Markham's *West with the Night*, the book Hemingway had unintentionally helped to revive, Gellhorn admitted to her regret at not getting to know Markham better.) Still, she was happy there like her former husband, and would have stayed on had she been permitted to. But when her landlord sold his African holdings, she was forced to move, and chose to abandon Kenya altogether.

To return to Hemingway and his African obsession, there is one book of his with a strong African element – a flashback about an elephant hunt – which we have mentioned only passingly (in the Introduction). Hemingway began his novel, *The Garden of Eden*, in 1946, long after he left Africa for the first time, and worked at it off and on for fifteen

Hemingway began his novel, The Garden of Eden, *in 1946, long after he left Africa for the first time. Though set in Europe, it contains a strong African element – a flashback to an elephant hunt.*

years, leaving it unfinished at his death. (It was tidied up and published only in 1986.) Thus it is certain that Africa continued to engage his imagination in the period between his first and second safaris.

Reading this strange, experimental book significantly changed my

ideas about the development of Hemingway's attitude to Africa. Like
Green Hills of Africa and "The Snows of Kilimanjaro," *The Garden of
Eden* is about writing and the difficulties of being a writer. Its young
protagonist, David Bourne, is staying in the south of France with his new
wife. As a counterpoint to the main narrative about a troubled marriage
which becomes a *ménage à trois*, David struggles to write a story within
the main story describing an elephant hunt he took part in when he
was only eight years old along with his father and a tracker called Juma.

At a time when the hunt is not going well, David hears the great
elephant moving about during the night, then sees it for himself and is
responsible for pointing his father and the tracker in the direction of the
elephant's trail. But he quickly comes to see this act as a betrayal of the
animal, telling himself, "My father doesn't need to kill elephants to live
.... I never should have told them and I should have kept him secret and
had him always and let them stay drunk with their *bibis* at the beer
shamba . . . I'm going to keep everything a secret always. I'll never tell
them anything again."[10] When they finally track the elephant down, his
father wounds the beast in the lungs and gut, and the elephant responds
by attacking and wounding Juma. Father and son follow the blood spoor,
and David describes how they find the elephant "anchored, in such
suffering and despair that he could no longer move." His father fires
again, twice. The elephant crashes down, but still he is not dead. "He had
been anchored and now he was down with his shoulder broken. He did
not move but his eye was alive and looked at David. He had very long
eyelashes and his eye was the most alive thing David had ever seen."[11] His
father tells the boy to shoot, but he refuses. Instead, the "limping and
bloody" Juma finishes the job with two shots into the ear-hole and then –

> There was no more true elephant, only the gray wrinkled
> swelling dead body and the huge great mottled brown and
> yellow tusks that they had killed him for. The tusks were
> stained with the dried blood and he scraped some of it off with

his thumbnail like a dried piece of sealing wax and put it in the pocket of his shirt. That was all he took from the elephant except the beginning of the knowledge of loneliness.[12]

David's growing love for the elephant – spelled out in much greater detail in the story than I have – is surely an outgrowth of Hemingway's own increasing sensitivity towards the animals that are killed in his books: the kudu in *Green Hills* that carries the "odor of thyme,"[13] and the lion in "The Short Happy Life of Francis Macomber," whose wounding and dying are told from the lion's own perspective. But David's identification in *The Garden of Eden* goes much further than those earlier writings. His guilt over leading his father to the great beast and his understanding that after its death "there was no more true elephant" show that by 1946, when he began this novel, Hemingway's attitude towards animal suffering during trophy hunting had already moved well away from the relative indifference of his first safari and towards the sensitivity of his second one.

In The Garden of Eden *Hemingway creates a story within the main story describing an elephant hunt in which the main character took part when he was only eight years old.*

CHAPTER 8

The Second Safari

I thought how lucky we were this time in Africa to be living long enough in one place so that we knew the individual animals and knew the snake holes and the snakes that lived in them. When I had first been in Africa we were always in a hurry to move from one place to another to hunt beasts for trophies.

ERNEST HEMINGWAY
True at First Light[1]

Before we went into the Tsavo National Park on the trail of Hemingway's second safari, while we were staying with Alwyn Smith on his ranch at Lake Naivasha we were offered the chance of seeing leopards. It so happened that leopards had been killing cattle and goats in the area, and it was necessary to try to shoot them by setting a bait. Baiting animals is cruel yet justified when the animals are marauders or, worse, man-eaters. But although leopards are my passion, and I am always extremely eager for the opportunity to shoot a live one with my camera, I had no desire to see one dead. Finally, on the understanding that no leopard would be killed, I agreed to accompany the leopard-baiting party.

In 1934 Hemingway reported on the general hazards of leopard hunting for *Esquire* magazine in the following dramatic terms:

> Philip Percival ranks leopard as more dangerous than lion for these reasons. They are nearly always met unexpectedly,

Philip Percival came out of retirement and agreed to lead Hemingway again on his second safari in 1953–54. © 2003 Earl Theisen Archives.

usually when you are hunting impala or buck. They usually give you only a running shot which means more of a chance of wounding than killing. They will charge nine times out of ten when wounded, and they come so fast that no man can be sure of stopping them with a rifle. They use their claws, both fore and hind when mauling and make for the face so that the eyes are endangered, whereas the lion grabs with the claws and bites, usually for the arm, shoulders or thigh. The most effective stopper for a leopard is a shotgun and you should not fire until the animal is within ten yards. It does not matter what size shot is used at that range. Birdshot is even more effective than buckshot as it hangs together to blow a solid hole. (Mr P. took the top of the head off one once with a load of number sevens and the leopard came right on by and on for fifteen yards. Didn't know he was dead it seems. Tripped on a blade of grass or something finally.)[2]

Twenty years later, in his journal about the second safari that became *True at First Light*, Hemingway described his own hunt for a particular leopard that had been condemned to die by the game department for having killed sixteen goats. He and his party spot the animal reclining in a tree, and his rifle shot knocks it off the branch onto the ground with a heavy thump – but then the leopard disappears into the bush, creating the most dangerous of predicaments for the hunters. Hemingway and his tracker Ngui follow the leopard's blood spoor. On the way Ngui picks something out of a clot of blood on the ground and hands it across: "It was a piece of shoulder blade and I put it in my mouth. There is no explanation of that. I did it without thinking. But it linked us closer to the leopard and I bit on it and tasted the new blood which tasted about like my own, and knew that the leopard had not just lost his balance."[3] An unnerving search in dense cover follows this discovery, until the wounded beast gives away its position by roaring, and is finally blasted to death.

As a leopard bait, one more unfortunate sheep was butchered and hung on the same tree as its three predecessors.

On our leopard hunt, we left at 6 p.m. to meet the trackers and gun bearer, who had been baiting leopards before our arrival. Over a three-day period, the animals had already consumed three dead sheep left as bait. They are clever cats, adjusting their habits to their own benefit and to outwit their baiters. Now, at the spot where a blind had been built, one more unfortunate sheep was butchered and hung on the same tree as its three predecessors. Our hope was to catch a glimpse of a cat or cats breakfasting at the tree early the next morning.

We ate dinner beside the camp-fire under a star-filled sky with the distant glow of lights on the eastern side of the lake. Around the perimeter of the camp-site stood a few umbrella acacias, while the air was heady with the scent of palm roses. (About a third of all the roses bought in Europe are grown at Lake Naivasha.) A couple of friendly dogs nosed

Leopards are clever cats, adjusting their habits to their own benefit and to outwit baiters.

about, hoping for handouts. Eventually we went to bed, replete with both food and well-being, feeling like Karen Blixen in her lovely book: "Here I am, where I ought to be."[4]

Joerg woke me in pitch darkness from a fitful sleep disturbed by hippos grazing and grunting outside the camp. The time was 4 a.m., and we left for the blind at once. It was deathly quiet there, until the dawn broke and the birds began to sing. At one point in the silence I was certain I heard a bird's alarm call followed by a deep, guttural coughing sound that had to have come from a leopard. But our luck was out – the sheep's carcass remained untouched. We would have to return in the evening.

Around 5 p.m., full of hope, we drove back through the hills and scrub to the blind. Nearing the spot it was obvious that most of the sheep had been eaten; only the head and feet remained. A leopard must have hit the carcass soon after we had left it in the morning. Having eaten its fill, there was now little chance the animal would come back. This was a great disappointment. However, I had only to recall episodes in *Green Hills of Africa* to remind myself that frustration is a natural part of hunting. We decided to sacrifice one more bait: a cow instead of a sheep. Then, as the sun was going down, we left the blind and ranged the plains in the golden light, seeing impala, eland, gazelle and a herd of forty or fifty rather menacing-looking buffaloes.

We returned when dusk was thickening into night. Deep silence prevailed as usual, until the night-time chorus of francolin, guinea fowl and a solitary night-jar started up. Then, just before 8 p.m., while scouring the vicinity with his night-vision binoculars, Joerg saw the silhouette of a cat at the base of our tree. By the time I could look through, I could glimpse only a large shape bounding away into the brush. Perhaps the animal suspected there was a blind nearby. Even if it had, we were not in danger, because a leopard is far too skittish a creature to attack a human in a blind. A lion would have been a completely different matter. If it senses danger, a lion will certainly attack a blind, even when it has already begun to feed on a bait. On one occasion Joerg remembered, seven lionesses discovered a bait some two metres up a tree. One lioness then turned and scanned the bush around her. Slowly she approached the blind and stood eye to eye with Joerg and two fellow hunters. Then the other six beasts came up as well, sniffed the outside of the thick brush cover and clawed at it. Although all seven eventually wandered away, when the hunters returned later, they found the blind had been completely destroyed and the bait left untouched.

In the end, we gave up the pursuit. We would see no leopard. That night, dining with Joerg's parents-in-law in their secluded paradise with the hippos grunting and the night herons croaking at the edge of the lake, Alwyn talked of the enormous adjustments Kenya had made and was still making after the end of colonial rule. Although he did not mention it, I could not help but reflect that the eclipse of big-game hunting was a natural part of this decolonization process – the passing of white dominance over animals, as well as over men, countries and resources. The sort of hunting that Hemingway did half a century ago is a thing of the past. Hence, perhaps, why I had found leopard baiting to be an unsatisfying, even distasteful, experience.

☆   ☆   ☆

When 'Papa' Hemingway at last docked in Mombasa in 1953, twenty years after his first arrival, his original white hunter, Percival, was in his late sixties, living in quiet retirement at his Kitanga farm, breeding horses and cattle. But Bwana Percival agreed to lead Hemingway on safari again. In *True at First Light*, the writer's regard for his old friend, who had the "customary look of a cherub with a secret joke,"[5] would be even more effusive than in *Green Hills of Africa*. He calls Percival "a very complicated man compounded of absolute courage, all the good human weaknesses and a strangely subtle and very critical understanding of people"[6] – whom he respects more than he ever could his own father. On the first safari, Hemingway had given Percival the nickname Pop, and now the older man took to calling Hemingway himself Pop, "which was in a way a compliment, lightly bestowed and deadly if it were withdrawn. I cannot imagine a situation, or, rather, I would not wish to survive a situation in which I called him, in private, Mr Percival or he addressed me by my proper name."[7] For a man who had lost or turned against so many

In Cuba Hemingway formed deep bonds with local people, men like Gregorio Fuentes, the model for Santiago, the fisherman in The Old Man and the Sea.

of the friends he had made as a young man, his enduring affection and admiration for Percival was singular.

Such was Hemingway's celebrity that, as well as his wife Mary and a rich friend from Cuba, Mario 'Mayito' Menocal, the safari was accompanied by Earl Theisen, a photographer from *Look* magazine, anxious to shoot the great writer with some impressive trophies. Then Denis Zaphiro, the young game warden of Kajiado district (the location of the first two camps arranged by Percival) and a keen Hemingway fan, paid a visit. Zaphiro saw Percival as a mentor, and he may have been the one to introduce Zaphiro to the Hemingways. In his thirties, good looking, aristocratic and disinclined to suffer fools gladly, Denis became fast friends with Ernest and Mary and joined the safari for most of its duration. In *True at First Light* he appears as G.C. – "Gin Crazed." G.C. often has a sociable pre-breakfast beer with Hemingway, who is happy when his warden friend returns to camp after touring the district, because "we had become a family and we always missed each other when we were apart."[8] They kept in touch after

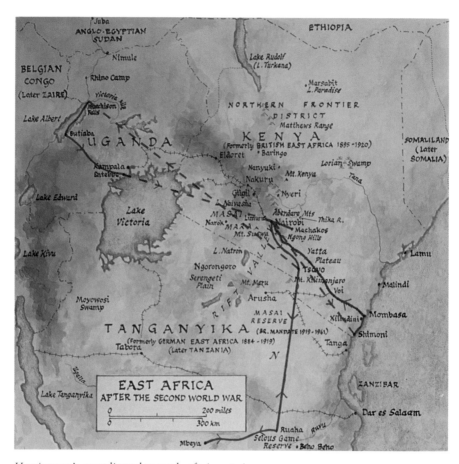

Hemingway's complicated second safari route in 1953–54

the Hemingways left Africa, and Zaphiro even visited Mary in America years later. As Hemingway presents him, G. C. is a complicated young man, with a more than usually difficult wartime career behind him, persistent insomnia which has made him exceptionally well read, and a strict code of conduct, particularly regarding involvements with the local women (not excluding Hemingway's own flirting). "He loved his job and believed in it and its importance almost fanatically. He loved the game and wanted to care for it and protect it and that was about all he believed in, I think, except a very stern and complicated system of ethics."[9]

The Hemingway party had been given permission to shoot in two game reserves south and southwest of Nairobi, first on the banks of the almost-dry Salengai River, then near the Kimana River and Swamp. The first camp was in a game reserve that had been opened exclusively for the Hemingway safari. Kenya's tourist trade – particularly the big-game hunters who Hemingway's stories had done so much to encourage – had been hard hit by the negative international press coverage of the violent Mau Mau uprising that began in 1952. The Kenyan government was eager to use the Hemingway safari as a publicity opportunity to encourage tourism.

When he first went to Africa in 1933, in the depths of the Depression, it is difficult to know from Hemingway's books and letters how aware he was of the plight of unemployed black Kenyans, though probably Percival talked to him about the poor state of the economy, in particular the failure of many farms started by white settlers. In 1953, however, he could hardly have avoided the anti-colonial unrest, nor would it have been wise to ignore it, given that he himself presented a high-profile potential target. A number of white settlers had been literally chopped up by the Mau Mau, and British troops were pitted against guerrillas in the dense forests. Only in 1956, with the capture of the Mau Mau leader Dedan Kimathi, was the uprising crushed, after the deaths of 63 European and 527 other members of the Kenyan security forces and 11,500 Mau Mau, along with numerous civilians, the great majority of them loyalists of the majority Kikuyu tribe from which most Mau Mau were drawn. "The Mau Mau years were very difficult, and countless atrocities were committed by both sides," wrote Richard Leakey in 2003, recalling the brutal killing of a great-uncle and his wife on the occasion of the Kenyan government's decision to honour the guerrilla leader Kimathi. "But from a Kenyan, rather than a settler, perspective, the Mau Mau did hasten the end of colonial rule – something that all Kenyans appreciate . . . In spite of our family loss during the revolt, I support the idea that Kenya should honour those who brought changes."[10]

Since Hemingway's safari was taking place in the traditional lands of the Wakamba tribe, who for the most part were not involved with the Mau Mau, Hemingway was relatively safe. But early in *True at First Light*, he records that his party had to take precautions against a rumoured attack on the Salengai camp by a group of Wakamba tribesman who had sworn a Mau Mau oath. The threat soon passes, though, and Mau Mau is not mentioned again in the book.

On their last day at this camp, Hemingway shot his first lion, the only animal he was really keen to bag during this safari. Local Masai tribesman had complained to Warden Zaphiro about cattle-killing lions and scavenging hyenas "as thick as grass."[11] Zaphiro set up a lion bait by hanging a hunk of zebra or wildebeest from a tree near a forest track. Two lions started to feed off the bait, but Hemingway's shooting was a messy business. He only wounded a lion, and it vanished into thick bush. Unlike the fictional Francis Macomber, Hemingway did not now bolt; but it took him and Zaphiro half an hour to track and locate the lion, which was felled with two more shots fired by Zaphiro, not Hemingway. This was not the clean killing the younger Hemingway would have made, nonetheless he was proud of it. "Watching the skinning, Ernest bent down and with his pocket-knife cut out a bit of the tenderloin beside the spine, chewed some and offered me a tidbit," wrote Mary, Hemingway's wife, in her memoir *How It Was*. "We both thought the clean pink flesh delicious, steak tartare without the capers. Denis [Zaphiro] scoffed that it would make us sick and Philip [Percival] politely declined a taste. In Kenya neither the natives nor the whites ate lion, having against it some taboo which they would never define for me."[12] In her book she went on to suggest lion-meat recipes, recommending that the slightly bland meat be "dressed . . . up with garlic and onion and various tomato and cheese sauces."[13]

In mid-September, the safari party struck camp and drove east into the Tsavo region to a new camp that Zaphiro had christened Fig Tree.

* * *

On our way to Tsavo National Park from Lake Naivasha we stopped on a whim in Karen, a suburb at the edge of Nairobi, to look at Karen Blixen's old farmhouse. The house has become a national museum with tourists poring over photographs and gazing at the famous view captured in the film of her best-known book. It was a wrench for Blixen to leave Kenya in 1931 after the collapse of her coffee farm and the death of Denys Finch Hatton. So much so that back in Denmark she could not bear to open any of her African boxes, stuffed with letters, books, pictures and mementoes, for over five years. Luckily for posterity, she finally relented.

Out of Africa first appeared in 1937 under her pen-name Isak Dinesen and was recognized as the work of an amazingly sensitive descriptive writer, who mixed careful observation with compassion in describing the places, animals and people associated with her farm. She could bring the world of her servants alive by quoting their conversation in Swahili mixed with English. The choice of words was hers but the sense remained

Karen Blixen's farmhouse, which she left in 1931, is now a national museum.

theirs, yet somehow comprehensible to the English reader. I am reminded of Joshua Mbowe, who accompanied me on my journey to the Nile and spoke English with the rhythms, images and philosophy of his Chaga tribe from the slopes of Mount Kilimanjaro. He once remarked: "Come with me and I will find what you are looking for. After that you can dance to the music of tomorrow."

Out of Africa is marvellous as a story too. The narrative seems to spill forth effortlessly – unlike in Hemingway's stories. Of course he is a good story-teller, but one never feels that narrative came fluently to him. He himself admired Blixen's writing enormously and paid tribute to "that beautiful writer Isak Dinesen"[14] in his Nobel prize acceptance speech in 1954. He even suggested that she and two other writers, Carl Sandburg and Bernard Berenson, should have received the prize before him. As he explained to his friend Charles "Buck" Lanham:

> You know I know more or less what category of writer I am but that's no reason to act swelled headed. Or tell anybody. And I learned a long time ago not to ever speak frankly or detached about it. Between us I was thinking like this: Sandburg is an old man and he will appreciate it. (He did.) Blickie's wife (Dinesen) is a damn sight better writer than any Swede they ever gave it to and Blickie (Baron Bror von Blixen-Finecke) is in hell and he would be pleased if I spoke well of his wife. Berenson I thought deserved it (no more than me) but I would have been happy to see him get it. Or any of the three.[15]

Karen Blixen was immensely flattered and told Hemingway in a letter that his appreciation gave her "as much heavenly pleasure – even if not as much earthly benefit – as would have done the Nobel Prize itself . . . It is a sad thing we have never met in the flesh. I have sometimes imagined what it would have been like to be on safari with you on the plains of Africa."[16]

What a strange fantasy! Surely Karen Blixen and Hemingway had nothing in common but writing. As personalities they were most unalike. Moreover, Hemingway got on famously with Bror Blixen, the husband Karen divorced. But then opposites do sometimes attract, so who knows? As our two Land Rovers bumped their way through arid savannah on the way to Tsavo, I found myself idly speculating on how *I* might have felt had I gone on safari with Hemingway. Leaving aside his big-game hunting and copious alcohol consumption, I think I would have felt uncomfortable with a man who needed always to be the centre of attention. But I would love to have been in Africa with Karen Blixen.

The sight of a vast giraffe graveyard jolted me out of my day-dream. In a land of predators and scavengers, death is never far away, but this field of bones, the relics of some of Africa's gentlest creatures, was strangely affecting. It looked like the work of poachers. Once someone tried to sell me a walking stick made of a giraffe's leg bone. I turned away, slightly sickened.

Just before we got to Tsavo, we drove through some lava flows known as Shaetani, from the Swahili word for "devil". The flows are very young, geologically speaking, only about two hundred years old. There are vast stretches of crumbled and shattered rock, incongruously black amid the green savannah of Tsavo. No matter how often I visit Africa, I am always awed by the startling diversity of its geography as well as its flora, fauna and peoples. The lava lies close to Kilimanjaro, and we decided to drive to the eastern flanks of the great mountain to watch the sunset. The sun dropped slowly behind the cloud-wrapped summit, its bright-yellow light shifting to orange silhouetting a few *kongoni* (Coke's hartebeest) which ambled, unconcerned by our presence, through the tall savannah grass in the foreground. The scene was a watercolourist's dream.

Our day ended chaotically. We had left setting up camp too late and had to struggle in the dark with tent poles while searching in vain for tent pegs, cooking utensils, soap, chairs – the usual safari paraphernalia – amid criss-crossing torch beams and increasingly fractious shouts. I made

Giraffe graveyard on the way to Tsavo – the work of poachers. In a land of predators and scavengers, death is never far away.

the discovery that campari and soda drunk out of an empty baked-bean tin tastes like nectar at the end of a tiring day. We turned in early; only the irritated monkeys at the bottom of the escarpment below our camp could be bothered to chatter.

✻   ✻   ✻

At Fig Tree camp, Earl Theisen, the photographer from *Look*, was getting restless for photos of Hemingway with his trophies. The new camp was a wildlife paradise, teeming with game just waiting to be shot. On October 1, during a morning walk to the bait tree both Hemingway and Menocal fired at a leopard. Menocal shot first, but Theisen, eager to take advantage of the moment he had been waiting for, persuaded Hemingway to pose.

His photograph is a classic Hemingway publicity image. White-bearded Papa, relaxed, cross-legged, sleeves rolled up, sits comfortably on the ground. His rifle juts skywards as its manly owner looks into the middle distance. In the foreground sprawls the inert body of a beautiful leopard – one that the hunter in the photo almost certainly had not killed.

For once the usually loyal – or at least acquiescent – Mary was moved to protest, as she recorded (long after Hemingway's death, it is true) in *How It Was*, her autobiography: "'It's wrong,' I contended. 'It is moral disintegration and desuetude,' I maintained with bombast. Ernest paid little attention to me. 'I'll get a leopard to salve your conscience,' he said."[17]

This pictorial fib is a good photograph, and when I look at it, though I feel sorry for the leopard, it amuses me to see Hemingway sitting so proudly with 'his' kill. But it is undoubtedly tangible evidence of the older Hemingway's willingness to connive with his adulators at some cost to his self-vaunted reputation for integrity. Presumably, he salved his own conscience by telling himself that his shot might have been the one that actually killed the leopard.

But Hemingway deserves credit for the fact that killing held less interest for him in 1953 than it had in 1933. With the exception of his lion and of Mary's all-important lion – the pursuit of which provides the narrative of *True at First Light* as the kudu hunt did in *Green Hills of Africa* – he apparently demonstrated no strong appetite for trophy hunting on his second safari. He was more eager to learn the animals' habits and watch the birds – something he felt he had earlier neglected in favour of shooting. When his friend Menocal and the photographer Theisen left Fig Tree camp for home, Hemingway was content simply to observe the wildlife, to explore the surrounding area on foot and to shoot chiefly for the pot.

Apart from her lion, his wife felt the same way, eventually concluding that her unfailingly inaccurate shooting, despite daily practice, was not so much the result of lack of skill but because "privately I couldn't bear to kill."[18] Her affection led her to adopt a baby Grant's gazelle early in the safari. She found it near a zebra carcass with no sign of its mother and at risk from predators, so she swept it up and took it back to camp, to be nursed on tinned goat's milk dripped through a cotton bud, christened "Baa" and quickly made into her darling creature. (When the time came to leave Africa and Baa, Mary was very upset. A woman from Magadi promised to look after the animal, but Grant's gazelles are notoriously difficult to raise in captivity and Baa was dead within a month.)

Having said all this, in Menocal's opinion Hemingway was discontented with his bad shooting and vented his frustration on his wife – a view supported by Bernice Kert in *The Hemingway Women*. If so, Mary, who was incredibly tough and forbearing throughout her marriage, refused to complain; and in other respects her relationship with Ernest seems to have flourished. In *True at First Light*, he writes of "the pride rising in me at beautifully sculptured, compact, irascible and lovely Miss Mary with the head like an Egyptian coin, the breasts from Rubens . . ."[19] And at the end of December, he wrote a strange diary entry for her, which she later published in *How It Was*:

> [Mary] has always wanted to be a boy and thinks as a boy without ever losing any femininity. If you should become confused on this you should retire. She loves me to be her girl, which I love to be, not being absolutely stupid . . . In return she makes me awards and at night we do every sort of thing which pleases her and which pleases me . . . Mary has never had one lesbian impulse but has always wanted to be a boy. Since I have never cared for any man and dislike any tactile contact with men except the normal Spanish *abrazo* or embrace which precedes a departure or welcomes a return from a voyage or a more or less dangerous mission or attack, I loved feeling the embrace of Mary which came to me as something quite new and outside all tribal law. On the night of December 19 we worked out these things and I have never been happier."[20]

Earl Theisen's photograph is a classic Hemingway publicity image – with a leopard trophy that the hunter has almost certainly not bagged.
© *2003 Earl Theisen Archives.*

This admission of gender-bending is frank, even for Hemingway. It plainly resembles scenes in *The Garden of Eden* where the young honeymooners come closer and closer in physical appearance, progressively blonder and more androgynous; not swapping genders but becoming the same gender. While Mary Hemingway allowed the publication of *The Garden of Eden*, she suppressed *True at First Light*. This may have been because the manuscript needed a great deal of editing, or it may have been because of Hemingway's scenes describing his liaison with Debba, the young Wakamba woman (whom we shall come to in Chapter 9). After all, her husband was simultaneously enjoying an older white woman pretending to be a boy and a young black woman who was sensually Mary's exact opposite. Since a lot has already been written about Hemingway and sex, perhaps it is worth noting merely that Africa seems to have had an unusually liberating sexual effect on him, as it has always had on certain outsiders, both male and female.

* * *

Tsavo is home to the Waliangulu tribe, the greatest elephant hunters in the region. In fact the tribe considers the elephant to be the only worthwhile quarry. In Hemingway's day, they were also the best-known trackers. The tribesmen have always been proud of the hunters and teachers who went before them, men legendary among the old colonial safari leaders like Bror Blixen and Denys Finch Hatton. They have not yet forgotten their hunting secrets, which they shared with us in talk, but they are no longer able to use them legally as a result of a long-standing ban on their hunting. Though their tracking tradition continues, I think it is likely to die out within a few years.

While Mary Hemingway allowed the publication of The Garden of Eden, *she suppressed* True at First Light. *This may have been because the manuscript needed a great deal of editing, or it may have been because of Hemingway's scenes describing his liaison with Debba, a young Wakamba woman. © 2003 Earl Theisen Archives.*

The Waliangulu are particularly known for their extraordinary back and arm muscles. The men are only some 172 centimetres tall on average, yet they are able to pull the string of a massive bow with twice the power of an old English longbow, and their poisoned arrows are able to pierce the thickest of elephant hide. The bow-strings are made from the sinew of a giraffe's leg, shredded, spun and entwined. Each Waliangulu bow is tailored to suit its individual owner. The poison was originally from the *acokaranthera* tree, and was made by chopping its branches thinly and boiling the slices for several hours. The basic recipe came from the Giriama tribe, Kenya's acknowledged poison experts, but certain species of euphorbia were also added to the brew, along with many ingredients from witchcraft. The Giriama favoured the innards of puff adders, the gall bladders and livers of crocodiles and usually a live elephant shrew, which is supposed to have the power to make a poisoned elephant stick to a path, making the wounded beast easier to track.

Naturally omens, good and bad, would be sought before a hunt. The call of a tinkerbird would be a sign of good luck, and the sight of a leopard tortoise an excellent portent; the hapless tortoise would promptly be cooked and eaten before the hunt set forth. By contrast, a hyena spotted as the hunt began would doom it to failure. After a successful hunt, the whole tribe would camp around the slaughtered elephant, skinning it with a special knife and removing tusks, tail and legs. They would either eat or make biltong out of the meat, which was seldom traded. The ivory, the feet and sometimes the tail and hairs, would be kept for trading.

In 1948, the Waliangulu hunting grounds were annexed into Tsavo National Park, and all hunting was banned except by licence, which the Waliangulu could not afford. Gobo Gallo Gallo, a Waliangulu tracker and gun bearer for one of Kenya's famous white hunters, Tony Seth-Smith, claimed to us that in his father's generation his people had hunted the elephant for its meat only. After the carcass had been eaten where it fell, the tusks were left lying on the ground. Later they might sell the tusks for just a few rupees – enough to buy clothing. In his own generation, the hunting ban has left no alternative but poaching. But Gobo Gallo Gallo insisted that "the bows and arrows could not make a big difference to elephant numbers, nor could European trophy hunting – they only took old animals for hunting. The real massacre was inflicted by the Somalis with their AK-47s. A bow and arrow could never have decimated the elephant population the way those guns did."

*　*　*

Hemingway's changed view of hunting brought an increased respect for the tribespeople he met. In his 1930s African writings there is an obvious lack of interest in the Africans as individuals. Characters like M'Cola and Charo in *Green Hills* make for comic cameos, but there is little genuine attempt to understand their history or culture. The Africans are the assistants to the real business – big-game hunting – and are used simply to flesh out the background to the white people's adventures. In this period, Hemingway shared none of Karen Blixen's sensitivity to local people.

But by 1953 the blinkers had fallen. *True at First Light* reveals the author's keen interest in the different tribes of the Tsavo area, particularly the Wakamba and, hardly surprisingly, the famously warlike Masai.

Until the nineteenth century, the Masai dominated the grassy plains that stretch eastwards from Lake Victoria almost to the Indian Ocean and southwards from the highlands north of Nairobi to the Masai Steppe of Tanganyika. Then, in the second half of that century, cholera and cattle diseases almost obliterated them, and the northern part of their lands were taken over by European settlers. When in 1883 the explorer Joseph Thomson had to cross Masai Land, as Kenya was then known, he held out little hope of a safe passage to Lake Victoria. The Masai *morani*, when he finally came face to face with them, were as impressive as he had imagined. "Passing through the forest," he wrote in *Through Masai*

Land, "we soon set our eyes upon the dreaded warriors that had been so long the subject of my waking dreams, and I could not but involuntarily exclaim 'What splendid fellows!' as I surveyed a band of the most peculiar race of men to be found in all Africa."

In *Happy Valley*, his account of the English in Kenya, Nicholas Best describes this splendour very well:

> Six foot tall, daubed in oil and clay, armed with shovel-headed spears and shields of bullock hide, they carried themselves with the aristocratic dignity of men who reigned unchallenged throughout the length and breadth of their world, and knew it. The Masai were afraid of no one, least of all a white man. Because they were not afraid, and could afford to be magnanimous, they had agreed among themselves to let [Thomson's] caravan pass in peace.[21]

By 1953 Hemingway felt that the tribe was a sad shadow of what it had once been. His wife Mary and Denis Zaphiro witnessed the cowardice of a group of Masai *morani* when faced with a cattle-killing lion. Zaphiro and a few of the Masai had tracked and cornered it and Zaphiro had gestured that the tribesmen should spear the beast. But they shook their heads. Zaphiro had to shoot the lion, sighing over what he called "Bubblegum Masai."

Hemingway blamed the tribe's demise largely on drugs and alcohol, but also mentioned their physique:

> The Masai had been coddled, preserved, treated with a fear that they should never have inspired and been adored by all the homosexuals . . . who had worked for the Empire in Kenya or Tanganyika because the men were so beautiful. The men were very beautiful, extremely rich, were professional warriors who, now for a long time, would never fight.[22]

Hemingway refers to the Masai, once a great ruling tribe of warriors and raiders, as being a "syphilis-ridden, anthropological, cattle-worshipping curiosity."

The Wakamba were among those who hated the Masai, and Hemingway took the Wakamba side, claiming that "drinking was as foreign to Masai as it was natural to Wakamba and they disintegrated under it . . . Some of the elders could remember when they were a great ruling tribe of warriors and raiders instead of a syphilis-ridden, anthropological, cattle-worshipping curiosity."[23]

Nowadays, like many other agricultural and hunter-gatherer tribes, the Masai are striving to protect their remaining lands and sacred sites, and, most important of all, their herds of cattle, which they manage with more efficiency than is generally understood. Milk is their everyday food, and in times when other kinds of food are scarce, they drink blood from the necks of their cows. Cattle are killed for meat only on special occasions, such as circumcision and marriage. They are rarely kept in larger numbers than the Masai actually need. But the governments of their lands have attempted to 'develop' and 'modernize' the Masai, arguing that too many cattle are kept in too small an area. The governments have also taken away their hunting rights and passed legislation against the use of their traditional weapons. The result is that, like the Hadza near Lake Eyasi in Tanzania we met earlier, the Masai are struggling to maintain their traditional way of life and secure rights to land that they have inhabited for centuries. They also want a fair share of the money they attract from tourists.

Today they must report to local centres, which has put an end to their nomadic lifestyle. They can still live in *bomas*, their dome-shaped mud-and-wood huts inside high, thorn-thicket fences which keep cattle in and predators out – but they must send their children to specified schools. Forced to stay in one place, the Masai have intermarried with other tribes, like the Chaga, and tend to live a more agricultural life. Such changes, which once might have been viewed as progress, may now be seen for what they really are: the end of a great warrior tribe. To see the Masai *morani* in their blood-red tribal dress selling souvenirs and posing for tourist dollars is heartbreaking to anyone aware of their proud history.

* * *

Hemingway's safari was now drawing to a close. From Fig Tree camp, he went south to Tanganyika to meet his son Patrick, who had bought a farm there in 1951 and was living on it with his American wife; Patrick was just then suffering a bout of malaria. Mary went back to Machakos to do some Christmas shopping until Percival received word from her husband; she and Percival then packed up the open hunting car and made the long drive to Tanganyika through lush forest into the baking desert south of Dodoma. After a happy reunion, the entire party, including Patrick and his wife, moved on to a very different landscape – the Bahora Flats of the Ruaha River. While Ernest lingered to do a little hunting, largely unsuccessful, Mary and Patrick drove to M'beya, the nearest provincial town, through thick rain forest. However the short winter rains were due, and soon the muddy road conditions forced a retreat.

So finally they all went north again, stopping for a week at Kajiado with Denis Zaphiro and then returning to an earlier favourite camp at Kimana Swamp. But with the coming of the rains, Kimana had become almost unrecognizable. Dust had turned luxuriant, rusty brown to lush green, and the place was alive with insects. For a while, somewhat to the alarm of his wife, Hemingway indulged his fantasies by turning native, going barefoot in the bush under the moonlight armed with nothing but a Masai spear, perhaps dimly echoing in his mind the exciting hunting scenes in René Maran's novel *Batouala* that had impressed itself on his imagination long before he came to the dark continent.

Then, it was time for him to leave the camp, never again to go hunting in Africa, except in the imagined world of *True at First Light*.

CHAPTER 9

Fact, Fantasy and Truth

We were going into the African world of unreality that is defended and fortified by reality past any reality there is. It was not an escape world or a day-dreaming world. It was a ruthless real world made of the unreality of the real. If there were still rhino, and we saw them every day while it was obviously impossible for there to be such an animal, then anything was possible. If Ngui and I could talk to a rhinoceros, who was incredible to start with, in his own tongue well enough for him to answer back and I could curse and insult him in Spanish so that he would be humiliated and go off, then unreality was sensible and logical beside reality.

ERNEST HEMINGWAY
True at First Light[1]

During 1954, the year he was awarded the Nobel prize, Hemingway began work on his "African Journal," an unfinished manuscript that would stretch to more than 200,000 words by the time of his death in 1961. His son Patrick, who had been personally present in the later stages of the second safari, in due course edited the original and reduced it to half

The first half of True at First Light *is about Mary Hemingway's obsession with finding and shooting 'her' lion. Her husband was torn between worrying about her erratic shooting and about her height. Eventually he shot the beast for her.*
© 2003 *Earl Theisen Archives.*

the size. In 1999, on Hemingway's birth centenary, after considerable argument among the trustees of the Hemingway estate, his son's version was published under the title *True at First Light* and billed as a "final novel" by Hemingway. The strange blend of fact and fantasy, the true and the false, in this interesting but flawed book about Africa, is well worth exploring.

Authenticity is suspect from the very first page. This opens with a short exchange between "the white hunter . . . a close friend of mine for many years" and "I." The white hunter offers a few words of advice: "Know everybody knows more than you but you have to make the decisions and make them stick"[2] – and then he departs the camp leaving "I" in sole charge. Yet when you turn the first page of the "novel," the white hunter is promptly named as "Philip Percival" and the reader is told without even a shadow of doubt that "I" refers to Hemingway himself.

Now it is known that while the Hemingway safari was staying at the Kimana camp for the second time near the end of the safari, Percival did leave for a period to attend to his family and farm business at Kitanga. Also certain is that Hemingway was left in official control and given the post of honorary game warden (though Denis Zaphiro, the real game warden, remained on hand); furthermore, during the course of his command Hemingway did diagnose and treat the illnesses of the safari crew and some Masai with antibiotics, did keep order among the crew, did keep watch for possible Mau Mau disruptions and did kill dangerous predators. But the version of these events he gives in *True at First Light* colourfully exaggerates his impromptu role as a safari leader. The opening scene sets the tone, in which the humble hero ("I") solemnly undertakes to keep everyone in the safari party safe until the great white hunter's return.

It may seem like a risky move for Percival to have turned the safari over to a man who was, after all, a writer not a professional hunter. But since the safari was static at the time, staying at just the one camp-site at Kimana, there was far less of an opportunity for trouble than with a safari on the move: no possibility of making, say, a costly error in an itinerary or a detour that turned out to be dangerous. We can easily assume that Hemingway could have learned, from watching his friend Percival over many weeks, how to lead a static safari.

The first half of *True at First Light* is about Mary's obsession with finding and shooting 'her' lion, an animal which has been condemned to die by Zaphiro because it is a cattle killer. Her husband worries that she may be turning a little "lion-wacky."[3] The whole camp is aware of the high priority accorded to Miss Mary's bagging the lion and in the "old straight way,"[4] without any motor car chases or other underhand tactics. Hemingway is torn between worrying about her erratic shooting and about her height – she is no taller than the tall grasses into which a wounded lion might retreat – and hoping that Mary will shoot the beast and make him proud.

Making Hemingway proud is a matter of no small importance in this particular lion hunt. His attitude towards his wife's quest is very condescending. He liked to play elder brother to her little brother, and Mary accepted her role. He was the seasoned veteran watching out for the innocent novice: "Miss Mary was a hunter and a brave and lovely one but she had come to it late instead of as a child and many of the things that had happened to her in hunting came as unexpectedly as being in heat for the first time to the kitten when she becomes a cat."[5] ("Kitten," like "Little Brother," was one of Ernest's nicknames for her.)

After weeks of tracking, anticipation and frustration, the killing of the lion does not pan out quite as Mary wishes. In a scene strikingly similar to Pauline's 'misfire' with a lion in the first safari, Mary succeeds in hitting her lion – "Piga, Memsahib. PIGA!" comes the cry – but not in killing him. It is Hemingway's bullet that breaks the creature's back, and a shot from Zaphiro that finally destroys him. Mary receives the congratulations, but is doubtful: "You're not just lying to make me happy?"[6] The same thing happened to Pauline. Little Brother may have made a valiant effort, but it is Elder Brother and his friend who save the day.

Or so Hemingway tells it. According to Mary, writing in *How It Was*, the lion did die as Hemingway describes in *True at First Light*, but she conducted the hunt with nothing like the demented determination he suggests. She enjoyed the attempt to lure the great animal into their clutches; it was a long and purposeful campaign; but getting the lion, she says, was never an obsession with her.

The second half of the book focuses on the Wakamba woman called Debba who is referred to as Hemingway's "fiancée." No one really knows how much of the relationship in the book is true and how much is wishful thinking. Nothing in Mary's own memoir of the safari in *How It Was* indicates that Debba was a threat – unlike Adriana Ivancich, the young Italian woman Hemingway had fallen for in Venice some years

Hemingway and Adriana Ivancich, the young Italian woman he fell for some years before his second African safari.

previously. Mary's only direct criticism of Debba is that she might benefit from a decent bath. When, one night, Hemingway holds a celebration with a group of Wakamba girls in their tent and the party grows so vigorous that Mary's cot is broken, she makes no comment when it is discreetly replaced.

Hemingway was a man who needed to be married. He also needed romance. It drove him and was also the engine of all his stories. In providing material for his writing, his romances were every bit as important as his he-man adventures. Mary apparently understood this and was tolerant. She knew very well that by the time she married him he was almost unimaginably famous, and could hardly have avoided the attentions of beautiful women even in the unlikely event that he had wanted to. Frequently, attractive intelligent women put themselves in his path – laughing at his jokes, showing off their knowledge of his work, displaying wide-eyed wonder at his exploits. Hemingway wanted to be loved and he wanted adventure. What better way to add an extra boost to a safari than a love affair?

Whatever may have actually happened between Hemingway and the nubile Debba, he made her a central character in writing up his "African Journal." He courts her according to Wakamba ritual, visiting her *shamba* (tribal village), bringing gifts and cultivating good relations with her parents. On the other hand, some elements of her behaviour in *True at First Light* seem like the fantasies of a middle-aged North American male, particularly her provocative impudence that so delights Hemingway. There is nothing she likes more than to sit in the car beside her fiancé and

> feel the embossing on the old leather holster of my pistol. It was a flowered design and very old and worn and she would trace the design very carefully with her fingers and then take her hand away and press the pistol and its holster close against her thigh. Then she would sit up straighter than ever. I would stroke one finger very lightly across her lips and she

would laugh . . . and she would sit very straight and press
her thigh hard against the holster."[7]

Later Hemingway learns that Debba is trying to impress the flowery
pattern on her skin, but his language is unmistakably sexual – not
to mention fairly ludicrous. Debba seems to find *all* of Hemingway's
weaponry exciting. At the end of a romantic picnic *à deux*, he shoots
three baboons, and when the killing is over, Debba insists on holding the
rifle. "It was so cold," she says. "Now it is so hot."[8] And when, after all
this flirting, the Wakamba elders decide that the two cannot marry, brave
Debba points to Hemingway's holster and says gamely: "I have all of you
in the pistol."[9]

If we judge from *True at First Light*, Debba was a greater cause of
marital discord than Mary's memoir implies. Hemingway's account is
suspiciously flattering to himself. According to him, it was not the
possibility of sex that bothered Mary but the idea that Debba might be
a rival for her husband's love: "I don't mind about your fiancée as long as
you love me more. You do love me more don't you?"[10] Mary's view,
supposedly, was that her husband was entitled to his "supplementary
wife" as long as she did not imagine she could "make you happier than I
can."[11] She was not angry at infidelity but anxious that another woman
might serve him better as a companion.

For Hemingway, Mary and Debba made the ideal combination: the
American wife who understood his fame, his mind and his writings, and
the African girl who knew nothing of his fame but embodied simplicity
and offered him the chance of more children, particularly the daughter
he had always wanted. Lying in his cot after a long day, he pondered
how lucky he was "to know Miss Mary and have her do me the
great honor of being married to me and to Miss Debba the Queen of
the Ngomas."[12] Hemingway's relationship with the two women was

*Percival left the Kimana camp near the end of the second safari with
Hemingway in official control and in the post of honorary game warden.*

apparently a variant on that staple talking point of African sexual freedom: the joys of polygamy.

Keiti, the chief of the safari crew, Mthuka, the driver, Mwindi and all the other Africans who had known Hemingway from his first safari with Pauline, believed that he was already polygamous. Not knowing that he had divorced Pauline, or indeed that by 1953 she had died, they thought "she was [my] dark Indian wife and that Miss Mary was [my] fair Indian wife." Hemingway did nothing to disabuse them, happy that polygamy was acceptable to them: that "Ngui, Mthuka and I could decide what was a sin and what was not."[13]

As the courtship of Debba grew more serious while Mary was away Christmas shopping in Nairobi, Hemingway became more deeply involved in tribal customs. He went through a series of rituals to woo her family's approval. First he paid the tribal price required to "sleep in the bed of my mother-in-law"[14] – in other words, several beers. Next he shot a leopard for his 'father-in-law,' as described in the previous chapter. He was even prepared to have his ears pierced and to make night patrols armed only with a spear. In short, he wanted to do "everything according to Kamba law and custom."[15]

One suspects that a good part of the courting was exaggerated in the telling. Born and raised in the mundane heartland of the American Midwest, Hemingway never lost a yearning for exotic locales and customs. Still there is a charge of genuine feeling here. Not so much in Africa, perhaps, but certainly in Cuba Hemingway formed deep bonds with local people, men like Gregorio Fuentes, the model for Santiago, the fisherman in *The Old Man and the Sea*. And for a writer, the ability to 'go native' is always a vital one in attempting to inhabit the characters one creates as deeply as one can. The trouble is, in *True at First Light* Hemingway did not try to penetrate far enough, and so the characters hover insubstantially somewhere between fact and fantasy.

It is therefore hard to know exactly what the book tells us about his second African safari. When I spoke to Patrick Hemingway about this, it was clear he regarded *True at First Light* much more as a novel (as announced on the book's jacket) than as a journal of record. Yet in his introduction he calls it a "memoir" and comments that "Ambiguous counterpoint between fiction and truth lies at the heart" of the book.[16]

Hemingway himself admits in the book that story-tellers make things up and are therefore congenital liars, and he justifies this: "I make the truth as I invent it truer than it would be. That is what makes good writers or bad."[17] But while plausible in relation to his other novels, his justification fails with *True at First Light* because the book mentions many people by their real names and describes many real events with what seems to be varying degrees of embroidery, distortion and gloss. The manuscript was written around the same time as Hemingway's memoir about Paris in the 1920s, *A Moveable Feast*. That book, too, has its share of exaggerations and omissions; but it stays more surely in the territory of autobiography, and its narrator's voice never pretends to be other than Hemingway's. *True at First Light* is much more nebulous than the Paris memoir. The "I" of the book has to be Hemingway himself – but Hemingway as he wanted to be rather than how he actually was. In consequence, sentimentality in the narrator, which might be forgivable or even endearing in a memoir, becomes cloying if we regard the book as fiction, while the righteousness of its central character, which might be acceptable in a novel, becomes unpalatable if we read the book as a memoir.

☆   ☆   ☆

Although the reader would never know it from *True at First Light*, Hemingway's second African expedition came to a catastrophic finish that nearly cost him his life.

In their enthusiasm for wildlife observation, the Hemingways began making low-flying excursions over the plains – "hedge-hopping," wrote Mary in *How It Was* (which now takes over the story). They were piloted by Roy Marsh, "a cheery spic-and-span young man who flew charter flights out of Nairobi in small planes." These flights were highly effective for game spotting. "In 1953 animals still lived in large numbers ten minutes by air from the little airstrip we had constructed – by running a car back and forth over our flat 1,000-acre front yard."[18] Although Ernest was initially nervous about flying so low, he was soon caught up in Mary's excitement and promised that he would take her on a special journey as a Christmas present.

On January 21 1954, after leaving Kimana and staying in Amboseli, Kajiado and Nairobi, they took off in Marsh's Cessna 180, stopping first at Bukavu on Lake Kivu and the next day flying north up the lake following the channel between Lake Edward and Lake George. The little plane went skimming over the lakes and came close to "bumping into hippos, buffaloes and elephants who had come to the shore to bathe and drink."[19] An overnight stop at Entebbe was followed by more lake skimming across the southern tip of Lake Albert, then over marshland along the Victoria Nile, until the party reached Murchison Falls – and disaster.

Murchison Falls is not a vast cataract like Victoria Falls, but it is a very powerful rush of water (as I know from photographing it at length in my pursuit of the sources of the Nile). The water gushes between high rocks down into a seething white cauldron. Spray billows up, obscuring the rock-lined depths. Below the falls, the Nile meanders in a lazy fashion towards the north end of Lake Albert, entering it a mere a few hundred metres from the lake's exit flow, where the White Nile begins its tremendous journey through the Sudan and the deserts of Egypt to the Mediterranean.

Danger lurks everywhere, whether it be from the thundering of the water that renders communication impossible or from the hippos wallow-

Murchison Falls, Uganda, discovered by Samuel Baker and named after a president of the Royal Geographical Society, is not a vast cataract like Victoria Falls, but it is a very powerful rush of water.

ing in the still waters above the falls. A single careless step anywhere along the riverbank can be fatal.

As Mary took photographs, the pilot Roy Marsh angled the Cessna to help his passenger get a better shot, circling over the cliffs and cascading torrents. Circling for the third time, he suddenly swerved to avoid a flight of ibis and ripped into an abandoned, almost-invisible telegraph wire, which sliced off the plane's rudder and radio antenna. Marsh managed to keep the machine, now rapidly losing altitude, away from the cliffs and careered towards the bush. The Cessna came down in some trees five kilometres from the falls. By an extraordinary stroke of luck, all three on board emerged relatively unscathed: Mary had two cracked ribs and was suffering from shock, Ernest had bruises on his shoulders, arms and legs, and Marsh was totally unharmed. But with the nearest village seventy kilometres away, their radio dead and the rumble of dangerous animals nearby, they had little choice but to rescue the last of the whisky, move uphill and pitch camp.

Worse was to come. Rescue arrived the next day in the form of a privately chartered boat, the *Murchison*, which took them to Butiaba, where Mary looked forward to a much-needed rest. But waiting in Butiaba was the pilot Reggie Cartwright, who had been scouring the area for the Hemingway party and was now eager to fly them to Entebbe in his twelve-seater de Havilland. Despite the landing strip at Butiaba being little more than a short, ragged patch of field, Cartwright was confident of a clean take-off. The engine started, the plane began to taxi, its tail bumped as it rose and then set down again, it rose again, then it nose-dived and burst into flame. First the right engine caught and very soon the fire spread to the fuel tank. The metal door frame buckled in the heat, but Cartwright, Marsh and Mary Hemingway were able to make their escape through a small window. Ernest however was too big to make it through the window and worked frantically to force the door open. The bruises on his arms and shoulders, still fresh from the first crash, made it impossible to apply enough force to the door, so in desperation he battered it open with his forehead. By this point, the aircraft was no more than a bonfire, containing their money, cameras and passports.

The party managed to return safely to the Railway Hotel in Masindi for several stiff drinks. Hemingway seemed to be holding up well, but the next morning his pillow was drenched with cerebral fluid. As a result of the two accidents, he had suffered a damaged kidney and liver, head wounds, burns, a dislocated shoulder, and the temporary loss of hearing in one ear and vision in one eye.

From Masindi they were driven to Entebbe, where Hemingway's son Patrick arrived with enough money to see them through the next few days, and went from there to Nairobi. Hemingway, concerned that Roy Marsh should not blame himself for the first accident, flew to Nairobi in

Hemingway's first plane crash near Murchison Falls in 1954. By an extraordinary stroke of luck, all three on board the Cessna emerged relatively unscathed.

Marsh's new Cessna to show how much he trusted him as a pilot, but Mary, too shaken from the recent catastrophes, could not summon the courage to accompany him and she travelled on the regular East African Airways flight. Even then she felt like "a sackful of terror."[20]

News of the crashes had already spread around the world, and the plane's passengers were assumed to be dead. In Nairobi, the severely injured Hemingway enjoyed the rare honour of reading his own obituaries, like his revered Mark Twain who sent the legendary cable to the Associated Press: "the report of my death was an exaggeration." Always fascinated by mortality, his own most of all, Hemingway immersed himself in the flood of worldwide eulogy. "He read and reread them enthralled," recalled Mary, "and gave no attention when I objected that the everlasting reading suggested unseemly egotism. After our day's and evening's guests had departed, he read in bed. Then, heeding my objections to the light, he read in the bathroom."[21]

Even by the swollen standards of the Hemingway ego, the obituaries were a bizarre *memento mori*. Moreover, they may well have played a part in Hemingway's receiving the Nobel prize. The Swedish Academy singled out for commendation *The Old Man and the Sea*, published in 1952, but the judges cannot have been unaware of the near-universal praise for his writing from the obituarists. As for the public, the two plane crashes and the courageous, not to say miraculous, escape from the conflagration made Papa Hemingway's reputation unassailable. Yet surely there is a certain vulnerability, too, in this unique vignette of a man compulsively reading about his own death far into the Nairobi night.

His behaviour now became distinctly erratic and volatile. He descended into slovenliness, holding audience with adoring visitors from his messy bed, constantly drinking despite the doctors' warnings, and lashing out at Mary. He knew he was acting abominably but blamed it on his mental concussion (as she herself did). On a fishing trip to the East African coast with Zaphiro, while out swimming with Mary Ernest attacked a nearby canoe, bashing it with a piece of driftwood – for which Mary sent recompense and apologies. Another day, while she and Zaphiro were away fishing, Hemingway, playing the hero, tried to help put out a rapidly spreading nearby bush fire. But the crashes had damaged his inner ear, so that when he rushed towards the flames he lost his balance and collapsed into them. When the other two returned, they found him sitting on the verandah, covered in burns, and had to send for urgent medical attention. In addition, his tribal fantasies acquired a deeper hold: he developed a fierce preoccupation with becoming a blood brother of the Wakamba, and began preparations to pierce his ears and scar his face. It seemed that the more difficulties he encountered, the more he retreated into the idea of a tribal world of simple kinship and belonging.

As already remarked, the crashes were entirely omitted from his "African Journal" and hence from *True at First Light* (though Hemingway wrote a jocular account for *Esquire* magazine). The omission fuels the suspicion that this book should be read more as wish fulfilment than as actual experience. In general, it has the air of a holiday in which everyday cares are put aside and modern frictions are banishable through the tough rituals of a purer and simpler way of life. The pleasures of the safari certainly come with their discomforts and their price, but this toughening up is worthwhile: "It was the stupidities of daily life with its unflagging erosion that was not worth what it cost."[22]

This new land of his imagination was a far cry from modern western urban life. Even its luxuries were different:

> Africans are said not to feel pain because they do not cry out, that is some of them do not. Yet not showing pain when it is received is a tribal thing and a great luxury. While we in America had television, motion pictures and expensive wives always with soft hands, grease on their faces at night and the natural, not the ranch, mink coat somewhere under refrigeration with a ticket like a pawnbroker's to get it out; the African, of the better tribes, had the luxury of not showing pain.[23]

Born and raised in the mundane heartland of the American Midwest, Hemingway never lost a yearning for exotic locales and customs.

African nobility, for Hemingway, was the antithesis of all that was superficial and superfluous in the West. In *True at First Light*, he tried to keep what was best about his western life while also adopting the tribal life. He wanted to have Mary and western literature and align himself with the tradition of the white hunter, and also have Debba and carry a spear and be close to the land and the noble Wakamba. This is what he had dreamed of doing in *Green Hills of Africa* twenty years before: to "really live; not just let my life pass."[24] In *True at First Light*, he insists, his Africa is "not an escape world or a day-dreaming world,"[25] but a world of ideals.

Which is why Mary's lion was so important and why Hemingway dwelt on it so much (even if she, in her memoirs, took a less intense view). It was not an obsession born of blood-lust but of "the absolute purity and virtue of killing a lion." For the Hemingway of this second African book, the pursuit of lions has become chiefly a spiritual matter.

Mary's "killing of her lion must not be the way such things are done but the way such things should ideally be done."[26] The lion may not die quite in the manner Mary and he desire, but it is the ideal by which she hunts that counts: the attempt to realize one's potential nobility in the face of elemental danger and fear of a kind that cannot be encountered in modern America or Europe.

*　　*　　*

If Patrick Hemingway's aim in publishing *True at First Light* was to enhance his father's literary reputation, then the plan did not work. This final posthumous fiction from Hemingway, following *Islands in the Stream* and *The Garden of Eden*, was greeted with sighs and groans from the critics. When *A Moveable Feast* had appeared soon after his death, it was hailed by all as an important document of an extraordinary period and by most as a beautifully written work. *True at First Light*, by contrast, seemed only to reinforce the convictions of those critics who felt that Hemingway did his best work before 1940. In their view, in later life he parodied his own hard-crafted style as success smothered his talent in self-importance and turned him into someone like his own prophetic creation, Harry, in "The Snows of Kilimanjaro."

I have sympathy with this criticism. But we should not forget that Hemingway never intended his unfinished, sprawling manuscript to be published. The version available in the bookshops today has been substantially edited and reshaped, not by the author. It seems reasonable to suppose that Hemingway himself, had he finished the book, would have rewritten sections, as well as cutting, honing and polishing the text. Hadn't he once told *The Paris Review* that he rewrote the ending of *A Farewell to Arms* thirty-nine times!

There are flashes of the old magic in *True at First Light*. Hemingway's eye for nature's beauty remains as sharp as in *Green Hills of Africa*, and the observations of animals on the move or seen over the barrel of a

gun are as vivid as before. But there are also sentences that run on and on, paragraphs that meander over pages. The deliberate repetition Hemingway was famous for using to reinforce subtle ideas in the reader's mind, is here too often wasted on pointless details. At one point, Hemingway reminds us that on safari, clothes are washed by hand and dried in the fresh air – a small, evocative touch – but then he adds, with almost comic banality, "Mary was washing with the safari soap and changing her shirt and smelling her fresh shirt that had been washed with a different soap and dried in the sun."[27]

There is a tendency in the book to pronounce rather than to observe, and to offer his habitual self-aggrandizement couched as humility. Thus Hemingway declares that he is no longer interested in killing beasts for trophies. Yet even as he writes this, he congratulates himself grandiloquently on a particularly fine buffalo trophy bagged earlier,

> which had a pair of horns worth keeping to recall the manner
> of the small emergency Mary and I had shared. I remembered
> it now with happiness and I knew I would always remember
> it with happiness. It was one of those small things that you
> can go to sleep with, that you can wake with in the night and
> that you could recall if necessary if you were ever tortured.[28]

The dialogue often sounds mechanical too, with everyone speaking in terse, declarative sentences. The exchanges of affection between Hemingway and his wife, which consist largely of each telling the other how lovely he/she is and how lovely Africa is and how lovely Pop or G.C. or whoever is, are particularly galling from such a fine writer.

But the hardest part of the book to swallow, at least for me, is not the stylistic infelicities but Hemingway's insistence on his contentedness. Of course *Green Hills* dwells on his contentment in Africa, but in that

Until the nineteenth century the Masai dominated the grassy plains that stretch eastwards from Lake Victoria almost to the Indian Ocean and southwards from the highlands north of Nairobi to the Masai Steppe of Tanganyika.

book the feeling springs from a highly alert and active consciousness. In *True at First Light*, the contentedness seems to have been bought at the cost of thought. Time and time again in the second book he remarks that Africa makes him happy because it empties his mind and frees him from responsibility. When, near the end, the romance with Debba is curtailed and Hemingway greets Mary's return from Nairobi, he admits that his happy state of mind depends on a deliberate decision not to think too much: "I put the other Africa away somewhere and we made our own Africa again. It was another Africa from where I had been and at first, I felt the red spilling up my chest and then I accepted it and did not think at all and felt only what I felt and Mary felt lovely in bed."[29] Too active a mind, too keen a sensitivity will not conduce to contentment, he implies. Hence, he explains, his heavy drinking: "I knew it was not just a habit nor a way of escaping. It was a purposeful dulling of a receptivity that was so highly sensitized, as film can be, that if your receptiveness were always kept at the same level it would become unbearable."[30]

During a bout of insomnia, Hemingway remembers a well-known line from his late friend Scott Fitzgerald's "The Crack-Up": "In the real dark night of the soul it is always three o'clock in the morning."[31] He sits up in the tent and thinks about the soul, recalling childhood experiences and worrying about what would have happened if the lion had killed Mary rather than the other way around. His thoughts are anxious, restless. But near the end of the book, he reassures us that he is not the worried, fretful type. The man who is at ease with himself has nothing to fear from the early hours, he asserts: "No man is ever really alone and the supposed dark hours of the soul when it is always three o'clock in the morning are a man's best hours if he is not an alcoholic nor afraid of the night and what the day will bring."[32] Which of these two men was the real Hemingway? Given the manner of his eventual death, by his own hand, the general tone of *True at First Light* seems untrue to the man. One feels that he protests his contentedness too much.

In Hemingway's two famous safari stories of the 1930s, Africa is a place where a man is forced by unfamiliar circumstances to confront himself, and he does not like what he sees. Their power derives in part from human psychological ugliness in the midst of astonishing natural beauty. Macomber, facing the lion, cannot avoid the fact that he is a coward. The dying Harry, facing Kilimanjaro, must confess to himself that he has betrayed his vocation for ease and comfort. In both stories, Africa is associated at least partly with conflict, failure and human (as well as animal) mortality. And the same struggles are also woven into *Green Hills of Africa* – in Hemingway's frustration with Pauline's shooting, in his competitiveness with Thompson and in his dicing with death at the hands of wild animals.

True at First Light fills out our picture of Hemingway in Africa, but does not really develop it. The earlier creative conflict gives way to harmony, but the harmony rests on a numbing of the faculties. The author is blinded by complacency, and so paradise is bland. East Africa had become not much more than an exotic retirement spot for an American literary lion burdened by his own success.

CHAPTER 10

Facing Mount Kilimanjaro

*I would come back to Africa but not to make a living from
it. I could do that with two pencils and a few hundred sheets
of the cheapest paper. But I would come back to where it
pleased me to live; to really live. Not just let my life pass.*

ERNEST HEMINGWAY
Green Hills of Africa[1]

It was an amazing dawn flight. Dazzling. We left Arusha airport at 6.45
a.m. Nearly thirty minutes later we were approaching Mount Kilimanjaro.
On the right we saw the jagged peak of Mwenzi and on the left the
stunning, square-topped peak of Kibo. As we flew directly into the blazing
light between the peaks, the sun itself seemed suddenly to shift, shooting
brilliant beams of light from the snow-capped heights, nearly six thousand
metres above sea level.

We circled the summit, past Leopard Point at the eastern edge of the
crater, around past the northeastern limits of Gilman's Point, then around
the flat, raggedy slopes of Shira and back again to the south side. Higher
this time, we made our second pass around the eastern edge of the crater
and Leopard Point. The great peak that appeared on our left over the
southern rim of the crater was Uhuru – the highest point in Africa. We made
our third pass, green tents visible below us. Then Kibo hut. Again we flew
between Mwenzi and Kibo with Uhuru peak to our left and there once

*In Africa, absurdly beautiful landscape is an arena for terrifying natural forces.
Mount Kilimanjaro epitomises this, and to contemplate Kilimanjaro is also to
contemplate the transience of human life.*

Our plane circled the summit of Kilimanjaro, past Leopard Point at the eastern edge of the crater, around past the northeastern limits of Gilman's Point, then around the flat, raggedy slopes of Shira and back again to the south side.

more was Leopard Point, poking up as a brown pinnacle from the eastern depths of the crater. For what seemed an eternal moment we were suspended over the centre of the crater, gazing directly into its depths.

Then we sped away. I became aware of a strange fuzzy-headedness and grabbed for the oxygen bottle. Within less than a minute, we were slowly descending, Kibo and Mwenzi already in the distance.

The Masai call Kilimanjaro "Ngàje Ngài," the House of God. I could now see why.

I had of course looked as closely as I could at Leopard Point, the place where Donald Latham had found the carcass in 1926 that had inspired Hemingway's story; where the leopard that had inspired me to follow Hemingway had wandered and died from cold. Now I had seen for myself just how high the intrepid creature had climbed and how far removed it had been from its familiar terrain. What it was seeking at that altitude was no clearer to me (or anyone else) than before. But why Hemingway had lit upon this specific image to open "The Snows of Kilimanjaro" – why the leopard had resonated with him – did seem clarified.

For Hemingway, I think the leopard's upwards exploration came to stand for artistic endeavour, even though, artist that he was, he chose to leave the symbolism unspoken. In journeying away from familiar terrain, the leopard was set apart from all other leopards, and though it died alone, it was not forgotten; its preserved carcass on the mountain is testament to its journey. Consequently we remember this leopard, and it intrigues us and causes us to reflect.

Hemingway must have seen himself in the leopard's rarefied ascent. The true artist, driven by unknown forces, breaks away from routine and embarks on an exploration of the unfamiliar. It is in making this journey that his name is preserved. Hemingway's compulsion to write and to write well, his desire to achieve the sharpest observation and the most enduring prose, was certainly in part a bid to cheat death. As he said of literature, if it is good, "many people remember you and they tell it to their children, and their children and grandchildren remember . . . And if it's good enough, it will last as long as there are human beings."[2]

Hemingway does not suggest that the artist can reach the summit. Only that, if he is serious about his art, he should attempt to get as near to it as he can. It is only when Harry, the dying writer in "The Snows of Kilimanjaro," recognizes this truth, however painful, that he is rewarded with a vision of the mountain's peak. Dreaming that the rescue plane is carrying him away, Harry looks out and "there, ahead, all he could see, as wide as all the world, great, high, and unbelievably white in the sun, was the square top of Kilimanjaro. And then he knew that there was where he was going."[3]

The linking of artistic pursuit and the search for immortality is hardly a new concept. But Hemingway's African context allowed for a fresh development of the theme. Perhaps this is because Africa, above all other places he lived in, was like a crucible in which a new life could be minted

The linking of artistic pursuit and the search for immortality is hardly a new concept. But Hemingway's African context allowed for a fresh development of the theme.

and lived to the full. In Africa, absurdly beautiful landscape is an arena for terrifying natural forces. Mount Kilimanjaro epitomises this, and to contemplate Kilimanjaro is also to contemplate the transience of human life. In a striking passage from *Green Hills of Africa*, Hemingway tells us – with a deliberately jarring mixture of mundane and lyrical metaphors – that "the worn light bulbs of our discoveries and the empty condoms of our great loves float with no significance against one single, lasting thing – the stream."[4] According to him, art is the one human creation that has a chance of resisting the stream.

But enough of metaphor. Africa, as we know, was a sensuously real land where Hemingway wanted to live to the full, and not just let his life pass. Looking back on my journey in his footsteps, I now think I came closest to his Africa neither during my leopard hunt, nor in interviewing people who knew him, nor while driving through his green hills. I was actually closest to it when I seized the country with my own hands and lived it for myself.

Waking in the very early morning, waiting for coffee and for the day to begin, offers Africa at its most sublime. On the last morning of my safari, by Lake Naivasha, I heard the morning chorus – the fish eagles crying to each other over the water, the cooing of the mourning doves, the hideous shriek of the *hadada* ibis and the melody of the African *bou bou*. Long streaks of sunlight cast equally long shadows through the acacias onto the glistening grasses and dark papyrus by the water's edge. Above me, the sky was a hazy grey, waiting to turn blue . . . There are few places on earth so idyllic. Africa in the morning promises the world. It is a place and a time where the idea of becoming one's best self and achieving one's best work seems attainable.

Hemingway achieved immortality through his best work; and part of it is African. As a boy he longed to go to Africa, and in his last years he longed to return there. Since his death, I can imagine that his spirit does indeed dwell, staining the white radiance of Eternity (in that phrase of Shelley, another romantic), near the top of Kilimanjaro – "as wide as all the world, great, high, and unbelievably white in the sun."[5]

CHAPTER NOTES

INTRODUCTION

1. Hemingway, "The Snows of Kilimanjaro," 3.
2. Donald Latham, "Kilimanjaro," *Geographical Journal*, Vol. 68, No. 6, December 1926, 492–505.
3. Jeffrey Meyers, *Hemingway: Life into Art*, 64.
4. Jeffrey Meyers, *National Review*, Vol. 38, May 23 1986, 44–45.
5. Hemingway, "Black Novel A Storm Center," *Toronto Star Weekly*, 25 March 1922.

CHAPTER 1

1. Hemingway, *True at First Light*, 19.
2. Bernice Kert, *The Hemingway Women*, 254.
3. Karen Blixen, *Out of Africa*, 224.
4. Nicholas Best, *Happy Valley*, 47.
5. Hemingway, *Green Hills of Africa*, 16.
6. Hemingway, "Safari," *Look*, January 26 1954, 30.
7. Hemingway, "Notes on Dangerous Game: The Third Tanganyika Letter," *Esquire*, July 1934, 19.
8. Theodore Roosevelt, *African Game Trails*, 37.

CHAPTER 2

1. Hemingway, *True at First Light*, 156.
2. Hemingway, *Green Hills of Africa*, 124–25.
3. René Maran, *Batouala*, 12.
4. Hemingway, *Green Hills of Africa*, 109.
5. Ibid., 231.
6. Ibid., 148.
7. Kenneth M. Cameron, *Into Africa*, 133.
8. Bartle Bull, *Safari*, 161.
9. Hemingway, *Green Hills of Africa*, 148.
10. René Maran, *Batouala*, 113.
11. Ibid., 158.
12. Karen Blixen, *Out of Africa*, 19.
13. Quoted in Ulf Aschan, *The Man Whom Women Loved*, 189.
14. Hemingway, "The Shot," *By-Line: Ernest Hemingway*, edited by William White, 419.
15. Hemingway, *The Old Man and the Sea*, 105.

Through all the adventures, travels, romances and achievements of Hemingway's early career, Africa remained a constant dream. He never got Africa out of his system.

CHAPTER 3

1. Karen Blixen, *Out of Africa*, 21.
2. Hemingway, *Green Hills of Africa*, 47–48.
3. Ibid., 44.
4. Ibid., 41, 42.
5. Ibid., 43.
6. Ibid., 95.
7. Ibid., 290.
8. Hemingway, "Shootism versus Sport," *Esquire,* June 1934, 19.
9. Hemingway, *Selected Letters, 1917–1961,* 432.
10. Jeffrey Meyers, *Hemingway: Life into Art,* 64.
11. Hemingway, "The Short Happy Life of Francis Macomber," 129.
12. Ibid., 132-33.
13. Ibid., 137.
14. Ibid., 137.
15. Ibid., 137.
16. Ibid., 145.
17. Ibid., 150.
18. Ibid., 148.
19. Ibid., 153.
20. Ibid., 154.
21. Ibid., 126.
22. Ibid., 151.

CHAPTER 4

1. Rolf Edberg, *The Dream of Kilimanjaro,* 91.
2. Hemingway, *Green Hills of Africa,* 155.
3. Hemingway, "a.d. in Africa: A Tanganyika Letter," *Esquire,* April 1934, 146.
4. Hemingway, *Green Hills of Africa,* 37-38.
5. Ibid., 72-73.
6. Ibid., 38-39.
7. Hemingway, "a.d. in Africa: A Tanganyika Letter," *Esquire,* April 1934, 19.
8. Bror Blixen, *The Africa Letters,* 197.
9. Hemingway, *Selected Letters, 1917–1961,* 541.

CHAPTER 5

1. Hemingway, *Green Hills of Africa,* 25.
2. Ibid., 83–84.
3. Ibid., 86.
4. Ibid., 5.
5. Ibid., 25.
6. Hemingway, *Selected Letters, 1917–1961,* 419.
7. Hemingway, *Green Hills of Africa,* 6.

8. Ibid., 11–12.
9. Stephen Dedalus in James Joyce, *A Portrait of the Artist as a Young Man*, ch. 5.
10. Michael Reynolds, *Hemingway: The 1930s*, 183–84.
11. Hemingway, *Green Hills of Africa*, 276.
12. Ibid., 239.
13. Ibid., 291–92.
14. Martha Gellhorn to Pauline Hemingway, January 14 1937. Quoted in Carlos Baker, *Ernest Hemingway: A Life Story*, 298.
15. Hemingway, "Notes on Dangerous Game: The Third Tanganyika Letter," *Esquire*, July 1934, 94.

CHAPTER 6

1. Hemingway, *Selected Letters, 1917–1961*, 408.
2. Hemingway, *Green Hills of Africa*, 12.
3. Ibid., 21.
4. Ibid., 24.
5. Hemingway, "The Snows of Kilimanjaro," 13.
6. Ibid., 16–17.
7. Ibid., 7.
8. Ibid., 20.
9. Ibid., 10.
10. Ibid., 9.
11. Ibid., 11.
12. Ibid., 11.
13. Henry James, "The Lesson of the Master," 188.
14. Ibid., 162.
15. Hemingway, *Green Hills of Africa*, 27.
16. Henry James, "The Lesson of the Master," 163.
17. Ibid., 195.
18. Ibid., 189.
19. Henry James, *The Jolly Corner*, 44–45.
20. Ibid., 24.
21. Ibid., 22-23.
22. Hemingway, *Green Hills of Africa*, 23.
23. Jeffrey Meyers, *Scott Fitzgerald: A Biography*, 272.

CHAPTER 7

1. Hemingway, *True at First Light*, 161.
2. Hemingway, *Green Hills of Africa*, 285.
3. Hemingway, "Notes on Dangerous Game: The Third Tanganyika Letter," *Esquire*, July 1934, 94.
4. Hemingway, *Green Hills of Africa*, 285.
5. Quoted in Bernice Kert, *The Hemingway Women*, 286.

6. Malcolm Bradbury, "It Really Is a Very Important Centenary: True at First Light" (review of Hemingway's *True at First Light*): http://www.users.dircon.co.uk/~litrev/reviews/1999/07/Bradbury_on_Hemingway.html

7. Karen Blixen, *Out of Africa*, 65.

8. Tom Charity, *Time Out Film Guide*, edited by John Pym, London: Penguin, 2001, 1022.

9. Martha Gellhorn, *Travels with Myself and Another*, 233.

10. Hemingway, *The Garden of Eden*, 181.

11. Ibid., 199.

12. Ibid., 201.

13. Hemingway, *Green Hills of Africa*, 231.

CHAPTER 8

1. Hemingway, *True at First Light*, 97.

2. Hemingway, "Notes on Dangerous Game: The Third Tanganyika Letter," *Esquire*, July 1934, 94.

3. Hemingway, *True at First Light*, 239.

4. Karen Blixen, *Out of Africa*, 12.

5. Mary Welsh Hemingway, *How It Was*, 362.

6. Hemingway, *True at First Light*, 13.

7. Ibid., 14-15.

8. Ibid., 138.

9. Ibid., 138.

10. Richard Leakey, *Daily Telegraph*, February 15 2003.

11. Mary Welsh Hemingway, *How It Was*, 346.

12. Ibid., 347.

13. Ibid., 348.

14. Telephone interview with Hemingway by Harvey Breit on October 28 1954, discussed in *Times Talk*, Vol. 8, November 1954, 12. See also Breit's front-page account in the *New York Times Book Review*, November 7 1954, quoted in Carlos Baker, *Ernest Hemingway: A Life Story*, 527.

15. Hemingway, *Selected Letters, 1917–1961*, 839.

16. Karen Blixen to Hemingway, November 1, 1954. Quoted in Judith Thurman, *Isak Dinesen*, 385.

17. Mary Welsh Hemingway, *How It Was*, 357.

18. Ibid., 358.

19. Hemingway, *True at First Light*, 252.

20. Mary Welsh Hemingway, *How It Was*, 369–70.

21. Nicholas Best, *Happy Valley*, 5.

22. Hemingway, *True at First Light*, 112.

23. Ibid., 180.

CHAPTER 9

1. Hemingway, *True at First Light*, 127–28.
2. Ibid., 14.
3. Ibid., 123.
4. Ibid., 26.
5. Ibid., 156.
6. Ibid., 166.
7. Ibid., 35.
8. Ibid., 144.
9. Ibid., 262.
10. Ibid., 225.
11. Ibid., 108.
12. Ibid., 281.
13. Ibid., 281.
14. Ibid., 269.
15. Ibid., 279.
16. Ibid., 9.
17. Ibid., 94.
18. Mary Welsh Hemingway, *How It Was*, 365.
19. Ibid., 376.
20. Ibid., 385.
21. Ibid., 387.
22. Hemingway, *True at First Light*, 271.
23. Ibid., 269.
24. Hemingway, *Green Hills of Africa*, 285.
25. Hemingway, *True at First Light*, 127.
26. Ibid., 157.
27. Ibid., 135.
28. Ibid., 98.
29. Ibid., 293.
30. Ibid., 176.
31. F. Scott Fitzgerald, "The Crack-Up," one of three essays published in *Esquire* in 1936, which appears in *The Crack-Up*, edited by Edmund Wilson.
32. Hemingway, *True at First Light*, 282.

CHAPTER 10

1. Hemingway, *Green Hills of Africa*, 285.
2. "Portrait of Mr. Papa," *Life*, January 10 1949.
3. Hemingway, "The Snows of Kilimanjaro," 27.
4. Hemingway, *Green Hills of Africa*, 150.
5. Hemingway, "The Snows of Kilimanjaro," 27.

BIBLIOGRAPHY

SELECT WORKS BY ERNEST HEMINGWAY

BOOKS:

Date of first publication is indicated in square brackets.

The Garden of Eden, New York: Scribner, 1986 [1986].

Green Hills of Africa, with decorations by Edward Shenton, New York: Scribner, 1998 [1935].

The Old Man and the Sea, New York: Macmillan, 1987 [1952].

"The Snows of Kilimanjaro" and "The Short Happy Life of Francis Macomber," in *The Snows of Kilimanjaro, and Other Stories*, New York: Scribner, 1995 [1936].

True at First Light, edited and with an introduction by Patrick Hemingway, New York: Scribner, 1999 [1999].

JOURNALISM AND LETTERS:

"Letters" in *Esquire* magazine: "a.d. in Africa: A Tanganyika Letter," April 1934; "Shootism versus Sport," June 1934; and "Notes on Dangerous Game: The Third Tanganyika Letter," July 1934.

"Safari," *Look* magazine, January 26 1954.

Ernest Hemingway Selected Letters, 1917–1961, edited by Carlos Baker, New York: Scribner, 1981.

WORKS ABOUT HEMINGWAY

Baker, Carlos: *Ernest Hemingway: A Life Story*, New York: Collier Books, 1988; *Hemingway, the Writer as Artist*, Princeton: Princeton University Press, 1972.

Edberg, Rolf, *The Dream of Kilimanjaro*, London: Heinemann, 1979.

Hemingway, Mary Welsh, *How It Was*, New York: Knopf, 1976.

Kert, Bernice, *The Hemingway Women*, New York: W. W. Norton, 1983.

Meyers, Jeffrey, *Hemingway: Life into Art*, New York: Cooper Square Press, 2000.

Reynolds, Michael: *Hemingway: The 1930s*, New York: W. W. Norton, 1997; *Hemingway: The Final Years*, New York: W. W. Norton, 1999.

White, William (editor), *By-Line: Ernest Hemingway*, New York: Scribner, 1967.

Selling cloves in the Tanga market on the east coast of Tanzania.

RELATED WORKS

Akeley, Carl, *In Brightest Africa*, New York: Doubleday, 1923.

Aschan, Ulf, *The Man Whom Women Loved: The Life of Bror Blixen*, New York: St. Martin's Press, 1987.

Best, Nicholas, *Happy Valley: The Story of the English in* Kenya, London: Secker & Warburg, 1979.

Blixen, Bror, *Bror Blixen: The Africa Letters*, edited and with an introduction by Romolus Kleen, New York: St. Martin's Press, 1988.

Blixen, Karen/Isak Dinesen, *Out of Africa*, London: Century Publishing, 1985.

Bull, Bartle, *Safari: A Chronicle of* Adventure, London: Viking, 1988.

Cameron, Kenneth M., *Into Africa: The Story of the East African* Safari, London: Constable, 1990.

Fitzgerald, F. Scott, *The Crack-Up*, edited by Edmund Wilson, New York: New Directions, 1945.

Gellhorn, Martha, *Travels with Myself and Another*, London: Penguin, 1978.

Huxley, Elspeth, *Nine Faces of* Kenya, London: Collins Harvill, 1990.

James, Henry, *The Turn of the Screw & The Lesson of the Master*, New York: Random House, 1957; *The Jolly Corner*, London: Martin Secker, 1918.

Latham, Donald, "Kilimanjaro," *Geographical Journal*, Vol. 68, No. 6, December 1926.

Maran, René, *Batouala: A Negro Novel*, [no translator], London: Jonathan Cape, 1922.

Meyers, Jeffrey, *Scott Fitzgerald: A Biography*, New York: HarperCollins, 1994.

Ondaatje, Christopher, *Journey to the Source of the* Nile, Toronto: HarperCollins, 1998.

Roosevelt, Theodore, *African Game Trails, An Account of the African Wanderings of an American Hunter-Naturalist*, with Illustrations from Photographs by Kermit Roosevelt and Other Members of the Expedition, and from Drawings by Philip R. Goodwin, New York: Scribner, 1910.

Thomson, Joseph, *Through Masai Land: A Journey of Exploration Among the Snowclad Volcanic Mountains and Strange Tribes of Eastern Equatorial* Africa, London: S. Low, Marston & Company, 1895.

Thurman, Judith, *Isak Dinesen: The Life of a Storyteller*, New York: St. Martin's Press, 1988.

A Hadza man lights the small L-shaped stone pipe that the tribesmen use for their ritual bhang *(marijuana) smoking.*

INDEX

*Forced to stay in one place the Masai have intermarried with other tribes, like
the Chaga, and tend to live a more agricultural life.*

*Previous page: Africa in the morning promises the world. It is a place and a
time where the idea of becoming one's best self and achieving one's best
work seems attainable.*

Kenyan workers on the outskirts of Mombasa play owari, *a count-and-capture bead game with many variations enjoyed throughout Africa.*

Overleaf: Kilimanjaro has had a mystical significance since the dawn of man.